MW00930279

My Heart for Safety

by

Joe Hopkins

Copyright © 2021: Joe Hopkins

ISBN: 9798756246049
Imprint: Independently published

Cover by Jackie Castle, www.jackiecastle.com
Cover photo courtesy of Fresh Air

Edit and Format by Lee Carver, LeeCarverWriter@gmail.com

All rights reserved. No part of this publication may be reproduced, stored in a retrieval system, or transmitted in any form or by any means, electronic or mechanical, including photocopying and recording, without the prior written permission of the author, except for brief quotations in reviews.

Table of Contents

PART ONE

Beginnings

Early Days

Jim and I had just pedaled our bicycles across town and parked them in the grass at the local airport. Jim, my first cousin, was my constant companion. The crosstown trip, about a mile, consisted of going down two hills, up two hills and across a creek and a railroad track.

The grass airstrip, one runway oriented east and west stretched in the sun. A dilapidated wooden hangar stood on the south side with a grove of trees to the north.

The main attraction, an airplane, waited proudly. Mr. Stultz had pulled his maroon Stinson Voyager out of the hangar and planned to go up and play among the puffy white clouds. "You kids want to go for an airplane ride?" In a flash we scrambled aboard and strapped in for a new adventure. An airplane ride! Wow! My first exposure to the world of aviation.

We flew through puffy clouds in a beautiful blue sky, a world I had never experienced before. We had to cut the ride short because my cousin and I had to get back home. I think that disappointed even the pilot. But I knew then that I wanted to go flying again!

My second exposure came at this same airport and involved a distant cousin who was part-time crop duster, part-time flight instructor, and almost full-time lazy man lying on an old beat-up sofa in the hangar office waiting for whatever might happen.

A school buddy and I became interested in aviation, so we decided to start a club. We recruited several of our friends and met at the YMCA. We had no instructor, so being the geniuses we were, we got some books and did our own discussions and study.

Back to lazy boy at the hangar. I started hanging out there quite a bit, hoping he would take me up in his Piper Cub. He would be glad to—at the rate of eight dollars per hour. Not rolling in dough at that stage of my life meant I would just have to save money from my paper route and lawn-mowing jobs. So that's what I did. Periodically, I would accumulate two dollars so he would take me up for fifteen minutes—just long enough to fly over town and do what everyone on their first flight wants to do—fly over your house to see what it looks like from the air.

During my non-flying times at the airport, I badgered lazy boy with questions about flying and how the controls worked. He let me sit in the cockpit all I wanted and experiment with the controls. Stick left, oh yeah, that's what the ailerons do. Stick back, elevator on the tail goes up. Yep, that will make the airplane climb.

Jim McGavisk and Frankie Hamrick, my best buddies, and I, grew up playing in the same mud hole together. Jim was also my first cousin, and we lived about a block from each other. In about 1950 Jim's dad, whose nickname was Army (and no one knew him by any other name) bought the first television in our neighborhood. I spent lots of time at Jim's house watching programs such as Packers football (Although Army was originally from New York, for some reason the Green Bay Packers was his favorite team), "Howdy Doody," and "Lights Out—The Shadow Knows." This latter one, scary of course, was on at night. Afterward my walk home alone on the road, so dark I almost had to feel my way, was terrifying.

At times, Jim and I were into building model airplanes—the balsa wood and tissue kind. Being creative kids, we occasionally would entertain ourselves by setting the models on fire and tossing them out of his upstairs window to watch them crash and burn.

We also did U-control models. These we built from kits as well. The model had two lines about twenty-five feet long extending from the wing tip to a hand-held control handle about five inches long, that were used to make the airplane climb and descend by pulling one line or the other. The lines connected to the elevator control by a bell crank located in the fuselage. The motor, a small air-cooled unit with a glow plug for ignition, used a special fuel concoction. We hooked a big 1.5 volt battery to the glow plug and spun the propeller with our finger to get it started. After starting, we disconnected the battery and the glow plug continued to provide ignition on its own by virtue of the heat of combustion.

Jim held the airplane until I got in the center of the circle, then let it go. By pulling the top or bottom of the handle with a twist of the wrist, I made the airplane take off, do climbs and descents, or even loops. All the while I was spinning around in the center of the circle having the time of my life and trying not to get dizzy. There was enough fuel for several minutes before the engine quit. Then I glided it back down for the landing.

Frankie's dad Walton was a budding pastor, and for a period of hard times they lived in a twelve-by-twenty-four-foot building in our back yard. Walton did fun things for us kids, such as applying removable tattoos and taking us to Raleigh for a college basketball game. Frankie's mom was a riot when telling funny stories at family or church get-togethers.

Another good friend was Ronnie Smith, our pastor's son. Ronnie and I once painted a fence on our property and, according to my mom, got more paint on ourselves than the fence. After preacher Smith moved to another pastorate, our new pastor, Rev. Reinert, came with a son also named Ronnie. This Ronnie had a woodburning set that I really liked, so I traded my bicycle for it, which made my dad very unhappy!

When I was about twelve years old, Frankie moved away because his dad took a pastorate in Bluefield, West Virginia. Jim and I decided to visit him. Unbelievable today, our parents allowed us to hitchhike from Draper to Bluefield and back—a distance of about 135 miles. Actually, I can't remember for sure if that was both ways. We may have ridden there with Frankie's parents and hitchhiked back home. I do remember that on one part of the trip back, a couple picked us up in an early 1950s four-door Ford, and the driver decided to show off a little by accelerating to almost 100 mph! And this was back before seatbelts. God's mercies are new every day. We arrived home safely and no worse for wear.

As a kid of probably ten or twelve, I was walking toward home one day when a car stopped and the driver, Kenneth Adkins, leaned out the window and asked if I would like a job delivering newspapers. I accepted, and for the next couple of years had several routes and delivered papers all over my little town of Draper, NC, population 3,500. I rolled the papers, secured them with a rubber band, and placed them in my newspaper bag, which was slung over my bike's handlebars. That way, I didn't have to stop but just gave the rolled-up paper a sling to the customers' porches as I rode past. Some days the early morning route was tough when it was cold or raining and I could not talk Dad into taking me on the route in the car. Poor me, but I guess it helped in learning responsibility.

My other source of income as a kid was from mowing grass. At first I used a reel type mower with an engine. When rotary mowers came out, I graduated to that type, being careful to not cut my toes off. The first rotaries did not have side guards.

Our house on Early Avenue had a fence around the property. One day dad surprised us with a Shetland pony, which we kept in our yard. It was brown and white and came with a nice saddle. There was a small shed in back for the pony. We enjoyed it for some time before it eventually got mean and cranky, and we had to get rid of it.

House where I grew up as seen 75 years later without fence or beauty shop. Note building behind house.

In addition to the 12 x 24 building and the small shed for the pony, we also had an old outhouse (the kind with a crescent moon carved in the door, and a one-holer, I believe) at the back of the property. Fortunately, we didn't have to use it, because at some point the house gained a bathroom. At the front corner by the street, my mom had a beauty shop that she ran for quite a few years. I remember that rats liked to hang out under the beauty shop. Dad had a Remington 22 rifle and I, at a very early age, liked to take it and see how many rats I could bag.

The house, at my first remembrance, was heated by a Warm Morning coal stove. My job was to make sure the coal scuttle was full of coal by the time Dad got home from work. If I forgot, it was punishment time—I even had to go out back and find my own switch for the administration of justice.

When I was about eight or ten years old, my parents decided to install a fuel oil floor furnace. The furnace was under the floor with a grate above for the air to come up and circulate through the house. One day, while it was being installed, the hole was in the floor with no grate over it. I heard someone at the front door. It was our pastor stopping by for a visit, and in my excitement and haste to get to the front door, I walked right over the hole and fell in! Imagine the pastor's surprise when he saw me coming, but then instantly disappearing down the hole. Fortunately, I was not hurt, but I sure was embarrassed.

The house had a fireplace in the living room with a mantle. The mantle became a significant focal point. That's where Dad placed the pack of Lucky Strike cigarettes he caught me with. He did not punish me. He just said, "If you are going to smoke, you are not going to sneak around to do it. You can do it here." Unfortunately, the next day while Dad was at work, I took the pack of cigarettes and went to the nearby woods. Big problem. I forgot to put the cigarettes back on the mantle when I returned. Another case of having to go out back and find a switch for another administration of justice. Dad could really make it hurt, too!

My grandparents on the Hopkins side lived on a farm in the Virginia mountains of Patrick County. The closest towns were Woolwine and Stuart, VA. For several summers while growing up, I was allowed to spend a couple of weeks at a time there on the farm with them. My Aunt Nancy and her two children would also be there. We had a ball. We got to help lead the two big Morgan horses to the creek for water after feeding time and milk the cows. We roamed the fields and played in the barn hayloft. We hoed weeds in the cornfield. We explored Grandpa's blacksmith shop. I even got to operate the horse-drawn mowing machine and hay rake.

We made our own go-carts (gravity powered) and would ride them down the hillside on a trail we cleared out for the purpose. It even had what we called Dead Man's Curve. There was nothing more fun than wiping out on our go-carts trying to negotiate that curve. The carts were very simple. A long piece of wood with an axle piece ran crossways at the back and another for the front axle that would pivot. We steered by moving the front axle with our feet. We even made our own wheels by sawing off circles of wood from a small log and drilling a hole in the center.

Kermit, an adult grandson who was a special needs person and had a speech impediment, lived with Grandpa and Grandma full time and helped with the farm work. Grandpa had a car but didn't drive, so Kermit did all the driving for them. He let me drive a short distance a couple of times. I don't remember the model year but the car had a hand crank for starting and vacuum windshield wipers whose speed was dependent on the throttle setting and thus the amount of vacuum available.

Church was a regular activity. In addition to the Sunday morning, evening, and Wednesday evening services, there were Saturday night youth meetings, mission conferences and homecomings. As kids, we had Miss Louise Sweeney as Sunday School teacher and, on Wednesday nights, Mrs. Dillon, who told us interesting stories including some about watermillions (melons).

We also had revival services. I remember one in particular. The visiting evangelist liked to illustrate sermons. While telling the story of the Old Testament character Jehu who "drove his chariot furiously," he jumped up onto a chair and started hopping across the platform. The chair broke, hilariously ending the illustration!

The church also brought in evangelists who had after-school events at the church. When I was nine years old, cousin Jim and I were attending one of these. The invitation was given, and Jim went forward. I did not, but wanted to. The next day's after-school session found me going forward also and receiving Jesus Christ as my personal Savior. That was April 24. On May 4, I was baptized. I have dedicated my life to His service ever since.

Since I grew up in a strong Christian home, the decision I made to become a Christ follower brought no radical changes. What it did was strengthen my resolve to live a Christian life. Dad always exemplified his trust in God's leading in his life by saying things like, "If the Lord wants me to do thus and so, He will work it out." Or, "If

God wants me to have such and such, He will provide." I have lived my life with the same basic attitude. This has taken a lot of pressure off my decision-making. I have historically committed things to the Lord with a "Thy will be done" and then prepared myself to live with the result. Although I must admit that on occasion I have allowed myself to get a bit uptight about a pending result.

I joined the band in junior high, and Dad bought me a cornet. My uncle Herbert Burnette played a tuba and got cousin Jim and me into a local community band. It mostly consisted of weekly practice sessions, but we also would play for the annual Easter Sunrise service at the cemetery.

In high school, I continued in the band for a couple of years. We marched in parades and performed at the football games. Then, to my mother's great dismay, I quit the band and joined the football team for a couple of years. As for positions on the team, I played end, guard and tackle—sat on the end of the bench, guarded the water bucket and tackled anyone who tried to get it! Actually, my assigned positions were half-back on offense and line-backer on defense. Although getting into a few games for a few plays, my performance was mostly as described earlier in this paragraph.

Mrs. Sledge lived across the street from us, a widow by herself in a huge house. She wanted someone in the house with her during the night, so arrangements were made for me to go over to her house at bedtime. I slept in a small room in the back of the house for probably a year before we moved away.

By the way, several years later, after being accepted by Mission Aviation Fellowship (MAF) for service with them, and returning to Draper for deputation, my wife

Elaine and I, along with our children Judy and Steve, lived in that same house as a family for a short time before leaving for Brazil. Mrs. Sledge had passed away, and the family was glad to have someone living in the house, so they provided it to us rent free.

Up through eighth grade we lived in the little town of Draper. Draper was near two other towns of Leaksville and Spray. (Funny story: A visiting evangelist held a two-week tent revival. It rained the entire two weeks. He changed the names to Leakville, Spray, and Dripper.) Together they were known as the Tri-Cities. But then they consolidated and changed the name to Eden. The new consolidated high school was called Tri-City High School.

As I went into the ninth grade, we moved from Draper to the central community. Our house was only one block from the new high school. I thought, "This is great. I can sleep late and walk to school." But suddenly life changed. I got a job as school bus driver at the ripe old age of sixteen. I made $22.00 per month. (Yes, North Carolina had student bus drivers back then.) However, I now had to leave home an hour earlier in order to drive the school bus route. I kept the bus parked in our backyard.

The buses had governors on them limiting them to a top speed of 30-35 mph. The first bus I drove was number 53. It was old and had a non-synchronous transmission which meant that I had to double-clutch it to shift gears. What that means is that when shifting gears, as I went through neutral going from one gear to the other, I had to let out the clutch, rev up the engine just the right amount to get the engine gear turning at the proper speed to mesh with the selected transmission gear, then shift into the next gear and let the clutch out. Got that? If I didn't rev the engine the proper amount, the gear ground loudly. After about a year, I got a new bus with a synchronous transmission that did not require double-clutching to shift gears—still stick shift, though.

Going back to Kenneth, the guy who offered me the newspaper job, he was also a ham radio operator. Another school buddy by the name of Leon Combs became interested in ham radio along with several others of my age group. This tweaked my interest, and I pursued it. After learning the Morse code and studying radio theory, I needed to go to Washington, DC to the Federal Communications Commission (FCC) office to take the test. My cousin, Leonard Hopkins, was a truck driver, and he had a trip to the DC area. I hitched a ride with him. He dropped me off and agreed to pick me up on his way back through. Details are vague, but as I remember it, I had a distant uncle who was a senator and arrangements were made for me to stay with him. Though foggy, I remember him taking me to visit the capitol, and we rode on the underground train. Anyway, I took the test, passed, caught up with Leonard on his way back through, and returned home. Soon, the FCC notice arrived in the mail indicating that I had been awarded the Novice amateur radio call sign of K4BKI, which I still hold current as of today. I upgraded it to Extra Class many years ago, which involved more advanced radio theory and Morse code proficiency of twenty words per minute.

Toward the end of my high school days, I was working in my dad's grocery store doing everything from stocking shelves, delivering groceries, cutting steaks and grinding hamburger, to running the checkout register. One day, "Stiffy" Law, the local plumber, came in and said he was looking for someone to dig ditches for him. (Stiffy was his nickname. Many others in our town had nicknames as well. My uncle Army McGavisk, Bad Eye Dishman, and Peg Leg Carter were a few.) Draper was putting in sewer lines. He would pay seventy-five cents per hour. I took the job.

Along with my buddy DeWitt Howlett, we practically dug up the whole town that summer digging ditches from the houses to the street. Usually it went fairly well digging the dirt, but one particular job was a different story. The ditch needed to be about four feet deep, but after getting a foot or so down, the earth became hardened clay and soft rock. We worked days and days on that ditch using heavy five-foot-long iron chisels and pick axes. Sorry, it was all manual labor back then. No motorized Ditch Witch to be had.

Another job gave me the opportunity to learn cabinet making. My uncle, Charlie Abe Nolen, had a cabinet shop, and I worked for him a while. I helped him build and install the cabinets. He taught me how to make a rolling pin for mom on the wood lathe, and how to cut a straight line across a four-by-eight sheet of plywood with an eight-point crosscut hand saw. I learned that an excellent nail hole filler is made by mixing household glue with the sanding dust from the wood being filled—gives a perfect color match. He was responsible, as much as anyone, for my cautious, safety attitude, because whenever I started to do something on my own, he invariably would stop me with his "Wup, Wup, hold on a minute..."

My uncle, Army McGavisk, was in the North Carolina National Guard, and he got me and his son Jim to join. We were about sixteen years old. We would go to the armory and receive military training in such things as marching and disassembling, cleaning, and reassembling the M-1 rifle. Also, in the summer we spent two weeks at Fort Bragg, NC. They taught us important things like using lemon juice in the mop water during KP duty for cleaning the kitchen concrete floor—it sort of bleached it. I enjoyed firing the M-1 on the rifle range and actually was pretty good at it. I also, probably because of my ham radio experience, was assigned as radio operator on the captain's jeep. One day they caught me in a no-no. I was asked our location over the radio, and I gave it to them. We had been instructed not to do that!

Since Uncle Army was in charge of the Motor Pool, I also got the drive the captain's jeep part way back home as the convoy returned.

When I left NC to go to the Moody Bible Institute in Chicago after eight months and twenty days in the National Guard, I was given a discharge since I was leaving the state. I thought that was the end of it, but not long after arriving at Moody I received a letter from the state of Illinois saying I had been transferred, and asked if I wanted to be in the standby or active reserve. I chose standby. I never went to a meeting and might have had one physical exam, but that was all. Imagine my surprise six years later, about the time I was graduating from the aviation course, when I received in the mail an envelope containing an honorable discharge certificate from the military. I had fulfilled my six years in the Army Reserves!

Moody Days

It's been said there are three stages in a kid's life. The first is when he confronts his buddy on the school playground by saying, "My dad can whip your dad." Stage two comes when, as a teenager, he says, "Aw, Dad, you don't understand." Stage three has arrived when he is talking with friends and says, "Now my dad used to say..."

In my last year of high school as I was pondering what I was going to do with my life, I found myself in a bit of a quandary. Dad always said that no matter what we do in life, we should have some Bible school training first in order to build a solid foundation for life's challenges. My other interest was in being a pilot, but I thought my nearsighted vision would preclude that. Put that together with my interest in amateur radio, and I concluded that I should look into becoming a radio operator in the Air Force.

About that time, Dad saw an ad in the *Moody Monthly* magazine about their aviation training program. He said, "Hey, you could go to Moody Bible Institute to get your Bible training and also get your pilot training." Bingo! I applied, but being late, the upcoming aviation class was already full. Moody said that since I already had experience in amateur radio, I should consider taking Moody's missionary radio communications course the first year and reapplying for aviation. The Bible subjects would be the same for both courses. Next thing I knew, at the tender age of seventeen, it was, "Hello, Chicago."

My first order of business was getting settled into the dorm. My roommate was Harold Beaty. Harold was in the aviation course and went on to serve with JAARS before his untimely death due to health issues. I'm guessing, but Harold was probably only in his late thirties or early forties when he passed.

This dorm on Wells Street was very old and still had direct current (DC) electricity. We all had to purchase inverters to convert the power to AC in order to use our appliances such as radios. Our room happened to be next to another room which used to be "the organ room" and thus it had AC to power the organ. Well, let's see. Hmmm. By drilling a hole through the wall from our room into that one and running an extension cord, we had AC! (Actually,

Joe studying at Moody Bible Institute 1959

I didn't remember this, but recently talked to the student who occupied that old organ room at the time. He reminded me that I did indeed do it. Knowing me, I have no reason to doubt it!)

After one year, I was able to get a single room on the seventh floor in Smith Hall which proved to be more conducive to my studying—and it had AC power.

After getting settled in the radio course, I gradually felt I should complete the whole three years. These years were filled with Practical Christian Work assignments such as street meetings, visits to Pacific Garden Mission and skits in churches telling how missionary radio communications helped meet the needs of isolated missionaries. I built several pieces of radio equipment with the most significant being a

Transmitter Joe built in 1959 at Moody Bible Institute

500 watt transmitter. It consisted of two racks, each being four feet high, with another one-foot cabinet for the antenna tuner. It weighed a "ton."

In addition to the amateur license I already had, I also obtained a First Class Radio Telephone commercial license, which at that time was necessary for one to work on broadcast station equipment. Austin Anderson was head of the radio department. My two final-year instructors were Franklin Swan and Warren Palmer. There were five of us in my graduating radio class: Robert Wright, Curtis Davis, Leon Hearn and Rodney Maisel.

Regarding the Practical Christian Work assignments mentioned in the previous paragraph, I remember one in which I was assigned to work with one of the upper classmen in his assignment with a group of black kids in downtown Chicago. He had developed a great relationship with them, but basically they were a kid gang made up mostly of junior high school age kids. They loved attention, and one way they developed to get it was to put on a mock fight on the sidewalk for all to see. I was there to observe one, and they made it look realistic. They were tackling each other and rolling around on the sidewalk. Fists were flying. People driving by or observing from a distance thought they were about to kill themselves! I imagine they were also wondering about those two white guys standing by and doing nothing to break it up. The kids themselves got a kick out of it and loved doing it. They managed to end it before the cops came.

For spending money, I had several different jobs while in school. One was as an elevator operator. Moody's Smith Hall dormitory had old elevators that were not self-operating. They were controlled by a brass handle for up and down, and the doors were manually opened and closed.

Another job required a uniform with cap. It involved pumping gas and doing oil changes at the Martin gas station a few blocks away from the Institute on LaSalle Blvd. There were no self-service stations back then.

A third job involved cleaning office telephones in the loop area of downtown Chicago. I would go into an office building in my white lab coat carrying my little box of supplies, just walk into the offices without being invited, and do my job—secretarial offices and big boss offices.

We were carefully trained in making the procedure efficient. There was a specific order. First, I would pick up the receiver and place a square wedge on the phone base so as to hold the button down and keep the phone disconnected. Then with a damp polishing rag, the entire phone handset and base would be cleaned. Next came the flat spatula-shaped metal wrapped with the polishing cloth, and it would be run around between the dial face and finger dialing ring. Lastly, the mouth and earpiece would be wiped with a disinfectant cotton swab. The secretaries especially liked that clean fresh smell. Lastly, the wedge was removed and the handset replaced on the cradle. Then it was on to the next one. There might be as many as twenty or so phones in one office, so I could clean a lot of phones in one afternoon and only go into one or two office buildings. This was good training for me in learning how to make every move of a procedure logical and efficient.

I had a couple of summer jobs while back home in North Carolina. One summer I worked as assistant camp director at Cherrystone Camp. Actually, I pretty much ran the place since the director was often an absentee director. This was a Christian camp I had attended while still in junior high and high school.

Another summer I loaded freight on the night shift for Roadway Express in Winston Salem, NC. That was when I bought my little James motorcycle for transportation. I lived with several other students in the dorm of Piedmont Bible College. There were two challenges that summer. One, my roommates didn't respect my need for sleep during the day and two, the night shift of loading and unloading trailer loads of freight did not suit me at all. But, hey, it paid $1.75 per hour.

With graduation from the Moody radio communications course looming in 1959, feeling too young to go to the mission field and still "having propellers in my pants," I went to Mr. Paul Robinson, Founder and Director of the aviation program, and told him I would like to consider taking the aviation training also. His response was that I would be spreading myself too thin trying to be a missionary pilot and radio technician, too. I assured him

Flight camper getting ready for evaluation flight

that if I completed the aviation training, my plan would be to go to the field as a pilot/mechanic and just use the radio training on the side as appropriate. He agreed to let me apply, and I was accepted for the flight camp evaluation.

There were twenty-four candidates in Flight Camp. By the end of the week of being observed from many different perspectives including playing ball, maintenance projects and introductory flight lessons, twelve were accepted into the course. I was one of the twelve—with a condition. I already had the required Bible and missions courses behind me so only needed the flight training the first year. The condition was that I must successfully complete the flight training and obtain the Private Pilot License in order to be able to join the others the following year. This would be done on a part-time basis during that year.

Let me go back to the final year of radio at the institute in downtown Chicago for some necessary details pertinent to this story. One day while checking my mail at the school post office, I noticed a certain girl. I found out that she was a nurse (RN) interested in going to the mission field. Hmmm. Always felt that a nurse would be an ideal wife for a missionary pilot.

One Sunday evening after riding my 125cc James motorcycle (top speed 45 on level ground) up Chicago's Outer Drive (it was winter and as cold as a mother-in-law's kiss) to a Swedish Covenant church frequented by many Moody students, I was introduced to this nurse. But her date, experiencing an embarrassing senior moment at a very early age, couldn't remember her name! One thing led to another, and Elaine became my girl. She was from Jamestown, NY and had taken her nurse training at the University of Rochester before enrolling at Moody. Her dad wanted her to have a profession, and her mother wanted her to have Bible training. Lucky me!

Now to continue. After acceptance into the aviation program, I was given the opportunity to live at the Moody-Wooddale airport as night watchman. I had a small room upstairs and a separate small kitchen area. The toaster was not the pop-up kind but instead had fold-down sides to place the bread near the heating elements. I had to watch it carefully. I didn't. Just then, Mr. Wertheimer, the chief flight instructor, arrived and smelled the burnt toast. Yelling up the stairs, he said, "Smells like a new bride up there!"

This and other factors led me to the belief that after living on my own for six months, having a new bride to fix my toast might be a great thing. Chocolate cake she would send me via the flyboys traveling from the Institute out to the airport for their flight training didn't hurt matters either.

Elaine Lamberson and I traveled to Jamestown, NY for our wedding scheduled for January 23, 1960. Julian Andersen, Moody airport caretaker, had graciously loaned me $100 for trip expenses. True to form, it snowed on the day of the wedding so Elaine, being the dutiful wife-to-be that she was, shoveled snow off the  church steps while I took the car to a garage to have chains installed on the tires.

After the wedding, everyone gathered at the Lamberson home for a time of opening wedding gifts, fellowship and saying goodbyes. My former pastor, Richard Smith, had come to perform the ceremony. My parents, brother, and sister also came from NC. Frank

Hamrick was Best Man and came along with his mother, Winona Hamrick. Well, it was time for Winona to perform. She regaled the group with her hilarious stories—especially the one about attending a ball game with her husband.

I can't believe we did such a thing, now that I look back on it, but we set off for our "honeymoon" trip back to Chicago about nine o'clock at night, in the snow, and with no idea where we would stop for the night. Naiveté of youth at its best! Since I had chains on the car, it didn't take long to shake the chase party. Before reaching Erie, we found a motel and checked in. It had been a long day, and we were ready for a rest.

Next morning, we were still in bed when there came a knock on our motel room door. To our surprise it was our wedding party friends from Chicago heading back. They had spotted our car at the motel and decided to pop in for a visit! They brought food. Elaine's mom had packed lunches for them, so they brought it in and we had a fun

Unexpected motel visit by wedding party!

time sharing. We have pictures! One more overnight along the way, and we made it back home to begin our new life together as husband and wife.

We moved into a thirty-five-foot trailer on Hank and Lil Cosman's farm in Elk Grove Village that we had rented from former Moody classmates Jack and Linda Mount. It was basically one room with a curtained-off toilet that one had to hand pump to flush. It was located just a short drive from Moody's airport.

I still can visualize our first breakfast there together in our cozy trailer home. Bacon and eggs on a beautiful oval, red-trimmed white porcelain dish. The dish resides in our cabinet to this day, sixty-plus years later.

Since I only had to show up twice a week and sometimes on Saturdays at the airport for flight training that first year, I obtained a job with Hollenbeck and Sather as a drywall finisher. Elaine got a job in an area hospital as a nurse. I tell people that I got through school "by the sweat of my frau."

I also had a side job working for a Moody graduate who had a small aircraft maintenance business at a nearby airport. His name was Peter Tanis. Yep, the one of Tanis engine heaters fame. Perhaps I shouldn't tell this, but one day he had a job working on a Mooney that had a cracked manual flap handle. It needed to be welded, but Pete didn't want to have to take the handle out, so he welded it in place right under the instrument panel. I stood by with the fire extinguisher and wet rags watching carefully where all those sparks went in the cockpit!

I also had a couple of part-time teaching jobs. Moody wanted the aviation students to have some electronics training, so they hired me to develop a course and teach my classmates. In addition, I got an evening school teaching job at DeVry Technical Institute as a lab instructor a couple of nights a week. Moody classmate Bob Matthews also worked there, so we would ride in to Chicago together two nights a week. Somewhere in the midst of all this, I also worked for George French in an avionics shop at the Fixed Base Operator (FBO) on the Elgin IL airport.

Tiring of the small trailer in short order, we moved to an apartment temporarily until a house owned by another Cosman family became available. This is where our family life began as we welcomed the birth of our girl Judy and boy Stephen. They were born fifteen months apart with Steve (as he later preferred to be called) putting in his appearance just a couple of days before my graduation from the aviation course in 1962.

I did get my private pilot license on time that first year. My second year in aviation was spent taking the Airframe and Powerplant Maintenance Training. This was a full year. I took the oral and practical exams and obtained my Airframe & Powerplant (A & P) mechanics licenses. My third and final year was full time flight. Most of my flight training was given me by Leo Lance, who had been on the field with JAARS (formerly, Jungle Aviation & Radio Service.) I also flew with Paul Robinson, Paul Wertheimer, Dirk Van Dam and Bob Rich. We started training in the Piper J-3 Cub, but then Moody bought the new Cessna 150 planes that had recently come on the market. Boy, what a funny feeling transitioning from flying from the rear seat of the Piper Cub to the side-by-side of the Cessna! During my training I got to fly, in addition to the Cub and Cessna 150, the T-6 military trainer, Cessna

170, Cessna 180, Piper Comanche, and Piper twin engine Apache. Moody also had an amphibian Sea-Bee but unfortunately, it was up for sale and I was unable to fly it. Cost? Four dollars per hour for anything under 125 hp and eight dollars per hour for anything of higher horsepower. No charge for the instructor.

Joe with the Link trainer at Pensacola Naval Air Museum

My training for instrument flying was quite different from today. Much of our training was done in the Link trainer. It was a crude replica of a small airplane mounted on a pedestal. It would pitch up and down, roll from side to side, and rotate. A "bug" on a table would track "ground" movements. We also practiced in an airplane by using polarized shades. A yellow polarized plastic cover was placed inside the windshield which still allowed the instructor to see outside. The trainee wore polarized blue lenses which allowed one to see the instruments inside the airplane but, due to the cross-polarization, one could not see outside. We sometimes also used a hood which was worn on the head and restricted the trainee to tunnel-vision. It was easy to cheat with the hood and take a peak!

I remember the challenge on my instrument rating check ride. The airplane was a Cessna 150 which only had one radio for both communication and navigation. It was a Narco Superhomer and only transmitted on about twelve frequencies. The receiver had to be manually tuned to either the navigation station (VOR) or the communication frequency. It utilized "whistle-stop" tuning that would insert a low level signal on the communication frequency selected so one could set the receiver to the transmitter frequency. The air traffic controller asked me to report passing a certain navigation intersection (fix). That meant I had to leave the communication frequency periodically, tune in the navigation station, verify whether the VOR indicator needle showed the intersection still ahead or passed, then retune the receiver to the communication frequency (using the whistle stop feature), until passing the fix. All the while, I still had to tune back and forth between the two navigation stations—the one I was tracking my course on and the other to identify the crossing radial identifying the fix. Years later, a typical radio installation would involve two radios for communication—good for hundreds of frequencies and only one setting to tune both the transmitter and receiver—and two separate navigation receivers so I could monitor the track on one and crossing radials on the other. Of course today, with GPS, all this is shown visually on a moving map display making it super-easy for the pilot to know exactly where he is all the time.

I left Moody after six years: three in the radio course and three in aviation. By then, in addition to my radio licenses, I had my Airframe & Powerplant Mechanic license, Commercial Pilot license, Instrument Rating, and Flight & Instrument Instructor licenses. I also had the Advanced and Instrument Ground Instructor licenses.

Here are some highlights from the training at Moody-Wooddale Airport. All three runways were grass. Due to being only three miles west of Chicago's O'Hare airport, we had to fly our traffic pattern at 300 feet above the ground. Typical then at other airports was 800 feet, more or less. These days it is more like 1000 to 1500 feet. When departing the airport to the west toward our practice areas or for cross-country flights, we would fly out "the corridor" between two broadcast antenna towers at 300 feet, then climb to whatever altitude was appropriate. The latter part of our training brought on the Advanced Cross Country (AXC) experience and what was called tactical training—the fun part.

The AXC consisted of flying across the USA to Fullerton, California to visit the Missionary Aviation Fellowship (MAF) headquarters. Here we were given the opportunity to get to know the mission and talk to the staff about possible future service. Hobey Lowrance also flew with us in the MAF training airplane (Piper Pacer) for an evaluation and to show us some of the training they give to their new pilots.

Part of the Moody cross-country enroute training consisted of low flying across the desert—one time we accidentally hit a cactus with the wheel—and mountain flying techniques. We climbed to fifteen thousand feet to see our fingernails turn blue from lack of oxygen. We were taught about air currents and the proper way to cross mountain ridges. We landed at large airports and tiny isolated airstrips. We even got in some instrument and night flying.

Once we flew to JAARS headquarters in Waxhaw, NC for a visit. This time with no instructor—just Ralph Jacobson and me in the Cessna 150. At JAARS I remember being impressed with the Helio Courier airplane when Merrill Piper gave us a demo ride and showed us how we could follow a fence at low altitude and make those tight ninety-degree turns at the fence corners. As I remember, they had no actual runway at that time but were using a section of dirt road.

During Tactical training, we practiced the "bucket drop," which was a technique developed by Nate Saint in Ecuador. By flying in a circle and lowering a canvas bucket with a rope, he made the bucket become stationary at the bottom of the cone and then lowered it into a clearing to give gifts to the inhabitants below. We also did a follow-the-leader exercise in which an instructor and student in each Piper Cub flew a loose tandem formation at low altitude. We took off, stayed close to the ground, and flew around the neighborhood and around silos and trees, making turns around the obstacles, and did touch-and-goes on all the runways by rolling the wheels on the runway, lifted off and did a tight turn-around (similar to a crop duster) to do the same thing on a different runway. All the while, we stayed no more than a quarter of a mile from the airport. Fun! Fun! Fun! As they say, "Don't try this at home."

One more story. It was Christmas of 1961, while I was in A&P training. Classmate Bob Matthews and I were talking and got the bright idea of renting a Cessna 172 from a local airport and flying to my home in North Carolina for the holiday. We went to the airport, got a checkout, and loaded my five-month-pregnant wife in the airplane with us and headed to points south. It was a beautiful blue sky day. Unfortunately, with the late start, we had to overnight in Huntington, West Virginia. The next morning dawned cloudy and dreary. The weather briefer at the airport said we had better get going right away because the weather would probably be getting worse. When we left Chicago, our agreement was that we would alternate. One would fly a leg and the other navigate, and vice versa. It was my time to fly and Bob's to navigate. Unfortunately, we got started along the wrong valley. Partly due to the airplane not being equipped with a directional gyro but only a compass which would not hold steady in turbulence, and partly because in West Virginia there are many valleys and ridges.

Okay, not wanting to return and start over, we decided to make a course correction and pick up our correct course, which would be verified by the river and railroad. Guess what. All valleys in West Virginia have a river and a railroad! While we attempted to verify our position, the clouds got lower and began to obscure the ridge tops.

Now what? We even discussed a controlled forced landing in a field below, but that did not seem too good an idea with a pregnant wife in the back seat. After wandering around dodging clouds and ridges and wondering how this would all turn out, we spotted a four-lane highway below. Glory!

Having driven from NC to Chicago numerous times, I knew that had to be the West Virginia Turnpike. I knew it would lead us to Princeton and Bluefield. We were able to maintain about 500 feet above the ground and eventually got to the Princeton airport. I knew a friend who lived there, gave him a call, and he graciously picked us up and provided a place to stay.

The weather forecast still didn't look too good, so I put Elaine on the bus to my folks in Draper. A couple of days later, the weather lifted enough that Bob and I were able to sneak out along the New River and through the gorge and arrive safely in Draper.

Christmas with the family was great and the trip back to Chicago was a non-event of which the details have been lost in my brain.

Going home to North Carolina for holidays and summer vacations was usually an adventure. It was a seventeen-hour trip since there were no interstate highways at that time. Usually there were several other students making the trip together.

Two stand out to me to this day. One was Vann Trapp. I always said he probably saved our lives. He constantly regaled us with his jokes and stories, which helped us stay awake on those all-night drives. The other was Gary Chapman. You probably know him today as the author of the *Five Love Languages* book. He was from Salisbury, NC. Gary has remained a good friend over the years, and I appreciate his ministry so much.

Getting Ready to Go

After finishing my six years of training at Moody, it was time to move to North Carolina to begin the next steps of our journey to the mission field. Elaine and I had already decided that Missionary Aviation Fellowship (MAF) was our first choice as our sending agency. We liked what we had heard from the likes of Paul Lewis and Jim Truxton as they passed through and spoke with the students at Moody periodically. But first we had to pack.

I bought an old beat-up trailer that had been fashioned from the rear half of a pickup truck. It needed new flooring, so a sheet of plywood did the trick. Getting the tail light working and a quick coat of paint finished the job. I obtained a bumper hitch for my 1956 Chevrolet Bel Air. The big 500 watt transmitter was first to be loaded in the front part of the trailer. Then all our other belongings were piled high and covered with a tarp.

All went well until somewhere in Ohio. As I crossed a railroad, I looked in the rearview mirror just in time to see the trailer drop down on its front end and flip upside down. Oh, no! The police came and at first accused me of not having the required safety chains across the hitch. It turned out that instead, the tongue had broken behind the chains, a combination of a rusty weak spot and the heavy load of the transmitter up front.

It was late in the day, but there was a service station close by with a tow truck to turn the trailer back right side up. Fortunately, a mechanic was on duty with welding equipment, scrap iron and know-how. In a few hours the repair was completed, and we were again on our way. Unbelievably, when we arrived in NC and unloaded, the only damage was a slight dent in the top of the transmitter cabinet. Everything was so tightly packed nothing could move.

My home church, Draper Baptist, had a missionary home they let us move into and live rent free while we did our preparations for the mission field. I got a job at the local coal yard bagging coal and driving a fuel oil delivery truck. One day I was given an address for fuel oil delivery and was told to not drive into the yard because it might be soft from the rains. Well, stupid me, I drove into the yard and nearly got stuck. By the time I got out, the yard was pretty torn up with ruts from the dual wheels on the delivery truck. My boss and the homeowner were very unhappy, and I deserved the tongue lashing I received.

We had to travel to California to the MAF headquarters for an evaluation and candidacy. After hitching up the trailer once again, we headed out. Crossing the desert in the hot summer was a challenge. First, there were the signs designed to scare you by warning that the next gas was 100 miles away. Second, the car had no air conditioning. This we attempted to remedy on occasion by putting a box of dry ice on the floorboards. Fortunately, the windows were open so we didn't asphyxiate from lack of oxygen.

Joe & family on the way to MAF in California

One evening near Flagstaff, Arizona we drove into a national park and planned to sleep in the car. What I had not taken into consideration was that the elevation was thousands of feet up even though it was desert. We about froze that night and couldn't wait to get started the next morning.

All went well at MAF, and we received our banana rating—we were now part of the bunch! On the way back home we stopped in Glenwood Springs, Colorado to pick up a 16mm projector that someone had generously offered us to use on deputation (visiting churches and friends for the purpose of raising funding for our support.) The film we used most was one called Conquering Jungle Barriers, which was made by Nate Saint before he was martyred in Ecuador. It was very effective. We also had a couple of slide presentations with recorded narrations that we used.

Based on MAF's personnel needs at the time, our assignment was Brazil. We had indicated to them that we had no preference and were willing to accept whatever they had for us. We were told we needed to raise $290 per month in support plus another $50 per month, for a total of $340 while we were living in the city of Campinas, Brazil for language school. Plus, we needed to raise outgoing expenses such as boat passage and for things we needed to take with us or buy in country upon arrival.

Headquartering again back in the missionary home in NC, we began our work of raising support. My home church signed on, as did Elaine's home church in Jamestown, NY. Other churches and individuals came alongside as well.

Meanwhile, I needed income for living expenses. I found a job at the Burlington, NC airport, which was ideal for building experience even though it meant a 90 mile round trip commute each day. I did everything. There was a small radio shop, so I did some limited aircraft radio work. I did mechanic work in the hangar. I pumped gas and gave passenger rides and did some charter flying for commercial customers. I did a lot of glider towing using a Piper Super Cub and developed good relationship with the very active group of glider pilots.

I had several students for flight instruction. Two stand out. They were a married couple and both wanted to learn to fly. The husband was a doctor and the wife an anesthetist. The wife progressed well, but the husband struggled. His brain could only process one part at a time. For example, on approach to land, he first had to learn to flare to stop the descent, but then the landing would go haywire. We worked on the touchdown, but then directional control on the rollout was a problem. He finally learned to land on the grass, which was more forgiving, but he couldn't keep it straight landing on pavement. This went on for probably fifteen hours or more of dual instruction with him still not ready to solo. Typical time to solo was usually eight to ten hours. His wife, meanwhile, was doing well and close to solo. She surprised me one day by announcing that she was withdrawing from training. She didn't offer an explanation, but my conclusion was that she didn't want to put her husband in the difficult position of seeing her doing so much better than he.

There was a rich young guy in Burlington who had purchased a new V-tail Bonanza. He had flown it to the Greenbrier Resort in West Virginia and got snowed in. After getting himself back home via other means, he asked us to go to West Virginia and bring his plane back for him. The airport manager and I flew up there in the Piper Tri Pacer. We called ahead and advised the folks at that airport that we were coming.

During our preflight inspection of the Bonanza, we noticed there were lots of dents on top of the wings that looked like hail damage. Inquiring of their airport manager, we found out that he had sent the line boy (now-a-days they are given the more sophisticated title of Aircraft Placement Specialist) out with a broom to clear off the snow. Finding that there was a layer of ice beneath the snow, he pounded the ice with the broom handle to break it up so he could get it off of the wing! Expensive mistake! It was not an airworthiness issue, so we flew it back to Burlington without any problem. Who knows, it might have flown a little faster with those dimples in the wing just like a golf ball.

After about a year of working at the Burlington airport, it was time to pack up and head back to MAF headquarters in California for pre-field orientation and flight training. For this trip we had sold the trailer and '56 Chevy, and obtained a white Chevrolet Greenbrier van. This was a blunt-nosed vehicle with a Corvair engine in the rear. It had windows all around. We purchased a mattress which fit perfectly on top of the rear seats with about a foot-and-a-half of clearance from the roof. Judy and Steve enjoyed the ride all the way to California on that mattress up where they could roll around, play, and have a good view outside. Safety? What's that? We'd never do that today in this age of enlightenment!

The cross country trip went well both ways. We could feed the whole family for one dollar at McDonalds. Burgers were fifteen cents—it took three—one each for Elaine and me and one to split between Judy and Steve. Fries and drinks were a dime each. A night at a Holiday Inn would set us back about nine or ten dollars a night.

Upon return to North Carolina, it was time to pack for the big trip. I obtained twelve, fifty-five-gallon drums. They had removable lids with a lockable ring around the rim. We lined the drums with large plastic bags. After packing a drum over full, we pulled the top of the plastic bag together, inserted a vacuum cleaner hose and sucked the air out. Amazing how much they would compress. With the lid on the drum, nothing on the inside was going to move around.

Glen Turner was a friend from church. He worked at the local lumber yard. I took my tool boxes and Maytag wringer washing machine to him, and he built sturdy plywood crates around them. The wood came in handy for various projects after arrival in Brazil.

Now I had to get all of this to New Orleans to put on the ship. I learned of an old ¾ ton stake bed truck for sale and bought it. I put two recapped tires on the front and loaded everything. I drove the truck to New Orleans but had to stop periodically to add water to the radiator. I found out later the engine had a cracked block, but it got me there okay. I drove to the dock, unloaded, and then went to a used car lot shopping to find someone to buy the truck. After about the third stop, I had a buyer. I had about $300 in the truck and I think I sold it for about $150. Overall, a lot cheaper than having to ship all that stuff from NC to New Orleans commercially.

Joe and family ready to haul our stuff to New Orleans

Mom and Dad, along with my sister Linda and her son Robbie, drove to New Orleans with Elaine, Judy and Steve. A dear friend of the family and former pastor at

Draper Baptist Church by the name of N.A. Thompson drove down to see us off. The next day we set sail on the Del Sud for a sixteen-day "cruise" to Brazil. The Del Sud

Hopkins family leaving New Orleans for Brazil in 1964

was a combination of cargo and passenger ship. It carried about 100 passengers of which 30 on this trip were missionaries.

The cruise was an adventure. Our room was at the front end of the ship. When we passed through the edge of the remnants of a hurricane, the seas were a bit rough and we really had our ups and downs. The kids didn't seem to mind, but it got to Elaine a bit.

About midday on a beautiful blue sky day the ship slowed. The crew has seen flashes in the distance and put down a lifeboat to send a crew to check it out. Turns out, some fishermen had

Bringing rescued shipwrecked fishermen on board

been shipwrecked on a reef and needed rescue. One had a broken leg. They were all brought on board and delivered to our next port-of-call.

Our waiter, Mr. Pete, was fabulous. If we inquired as to what a certain strange-sounding menu item was, he would say, "I'll bring you some." He was always pleasant and helpful.

One day, while a group of us were out visiting by the pool, there was a commotion. Our daughter Judy had fallen in and one of the missionary wives saw her hair floating on top of the water. Diving in immediately, she rescued her before any harm was done.

A tradition in those days was to have an initiation party for any passengers who were crossing the equator for the first time. The ship's crew made a big deal out of it with Neptune decorations and rituals. It was a fun time. I think we were even awarded a certificate.

One night out on the deck, I was standing next to the captain. He pointed to some faint lights in the distance and said that they were on the coast of Brazil. I thought I'd better not, but wanted to call him a liar because Brazil was the mission field and there couldn't be any lights there!

The sixteenth day arrived, and as we were entering the mission field port of Santos, I was surprised to see a huge billboard on shore saying, "Frigidaire of Brazil welcomes you." My first of several culture shocks to come.

Paul Lewis met us at the dock and took us under his wing. First stop was a Brazilian restaurant where I was introduced to steak *a cavalo*. It was a steak with a fried egg on top, which turned out to be a favorite of mine. He took us to Campinas, where we would be living for the next year while studying the language at the *Escola de Portuguez e Orientacão*, or School of Portuguese and Orientation. He helped us find a house to rent and took us downtown to the Sears store to buy some basic furniture—beds and such. My second culture shock. Sears? In Brazil? This can't be.

After a couple of days, Paul and I had to return to the port in Santos to get our things through customs. My hopes that we would not have to open the drums were dashed. Every single one had to be opened. I thought, how am I going to get the lids back on without a vacuum cleaner?

It's funny now though not then, but we had been told by other missionaries in the States that sanitary napkins (Kotex) would not be available in Brazil, so we had purchased a case or two to take with us. The pads turned out to be great packing/padding material, but when the barrels were opened and the agent started poking through the contents—well, you can imagine that sanitary napkins, spread out all over the dock from one end to the other, was a sight to behold. The bewildered customs agent finally finished and gave us the go-ahead. We did manage, with difficulty, to get the lids back on. We hired a truck to deliver our stuff to Campinas and went on our way.

Language School

The purpose of language school was not only to help us learn the language but also some of Brazil's culture and customs. It was a good experience. Brazil is the only country in South America that speaks Portuguese. The others speak Spanish. Someone said that Portuguese sounds like Spanish with a French accent. That's not too far from the truth. It has a nasalized sound that takes some effort to learn. Some Spanish and Portuguese words are the same, some are similar and some are completely different. This made it difficult for me in later years to keep them straight when traveling back to Brazil or to other countries that spoke Spanish.

Spiritist meeting

One of our culture exposures during school was to observe a Spiritist meeting. It seemed weird, as you might imagine, and I didn't understand anything that was going on.

Another culture exposure was to attend the São João (St. John's Day) celebration. This included watching Brazilians walk barefooted across a bed of hot coals. I got pictures. One of the missionaries asked how it was done. The response was that one had to have faith. The missionary said, "I have faith," took off his shoes, and walked across. As I remember, he might have had one little burn spot or blister. They say the key is to keep your toes together and keep moving. I'm content to take their word for it without giving it a try.

My background growing up was along the lines of

Walking the hot coals

the adage, "I don't smoke, I don't chew, and I don't go with girls that do—I ain't got no girlfriend." Also, Christians did not attend movies. That changed. A couple we were close to in language school said the movie *Sound of Music* would be playing in the local theater. Would we like to go see it with them? Putting early upbringing aside, we agreed to go and enjoyed it very much. It was a great movie.

Graduation from language school came, and it was time to pack once again for our move to the MAF base in Anápolis, located 75 miles west of Brasilia (Brazil's new capital) in the center of the country at an elevation of 3,500 feet. The climate was pleasant year round. We did have a fireplace to ease the chill on those few rainy, cool days of winter.

Operational at Last

Irmãos Mosca. Translated, that means The Fly Brothers. That was the trucking company hired to move us from Campinas to our new home at the MAF base in Anápolis in 1965.

Two other families were based there. Frank and Jan Gibbs lived in a duplex, and Jim and Darlene Lomheim had a house next to the one we had been assigned. Frank was a full-time aircraft mechanic, and Jim was a pilot and Program Manager. Paul and Jackie Lewis (Paul was the one who met us upon arrival in the country) had returned to the States for furlough, so we were living in their house and using their Jeep Rural. Oh yes, and feeding their dog. That dog, a German Shepard, had an uncanny ability to know whether the person arriving on the base was a Brazilian or American. He barked at the Brazilians. Also, living close by was Manduka and wife, who was hired to help in the hangar. In addition, there was a fuel storage building and another small building where Jim Lomheim had set up a photography lab. I took advantage of that by developing and mounting my own Ektachrome slides. We also did black and white photos.

After years of schooling, training and other preparation, it was good to finally be on the mission field and in place for service as a missionary pilot. I looked forward to providing transportation for the missionaries into and out of their village assignments, any needed medical or emergency flights, and taking in their mail and supplies. All these tasks contributed to getting the good news of the Gospel to those who needed to hear. The airplane was and is a great tool for saving the missionary precious travel time, ensuring that they arrive safely and rested.

Aircraft at MAF base in Anápolis Brazil

The Presbyterian mission had a couple of airplanes, but their pilot was returning to the States for furlough. So my first assignment was to go on loan to them for a year. They had a Cessna 182, which was the one I would fly most of the time. It's the one in the picture with ASAS DA FE painted on the side, which means wings of faith. They also had a Piper Comanche which I flew on occasion. Before the year was over, they sold the Piper and bought a Cessna 206. For those readers unfamiliar with aircraft, the 182 was a high wing airplane and had four seats. The Comanche was a 4-seater, low wing airplane with retractable landing gear. The 206 was a high wing with six seats and a large cargo door on the right rear side.

These were not the only airplanes I flew during my time in Brazil. MAF had a Cessna 180 (high wing with seating basically for 4 or 5) which I flew some, mostly on flights to the west to the Cuiabá area to service the missionaries out near the Bolivian border. Another

Piper Pacer rebuild – Noel Willems painting

Presbyterian mission had a Cessna 172 (high wing, low horsepower) which I flew very little. Last, but not least, when we moved from the base in Anápolis to São Luís on the northeast coast, I flew a Piper Pacer. The Pacer is a "rag-covered" steel frame, high wing airplane with four seats. It had just undergone an extensive rebuild and refurbishment at the MAF overhaul center in Anápolis.

My on-loan assignment to the Presbyterians consisted mostly of taking two of their missionaries on long weekend trips up north to visit their national pastors, who were serving newly formed churches along the Brasilia to Belem highway. I use the term highway loosely since the dirt road was new, rough, and very muddy in the rainy season. New communities were forming along the highway so the mission was dedicated to getting new churches established to serve the people. Typically, we would leave on Thursday with both missionaries aboard. I would drop one of them off at the first stop and continue on to the next town where I would overnight with the second missionary. The next day I would go back and pick up the first missionary, and we would repeat the process at two more towns for the second night. Weather permitting, we would make it back home on Monday.

At that time, due to the political situation in Brazil, the mission planes were not allowed to use communication radios except for air traffic control purposes. Nor could missionaries out in the bush use a radio. Therefore, I would kiss the wife goodbye on Thursday and tell her I would see her Monday, "If we don't have a problem with the weather." I would be somewhere between 400 and 700 miles away from home without any communications with home base for the entire weekend! In today's missionary aviation world, that would be unheard of. An inoperable radio today generally means the aircraft "ain't going nowhere."

Usually the weather cooperated fairly well on these flights, but occasionally I would have to deviate to an alternate. On one occasion, it had rained really hard at my destination airstrip, and as I circled I could see water standing on the runway. I continued circling for about

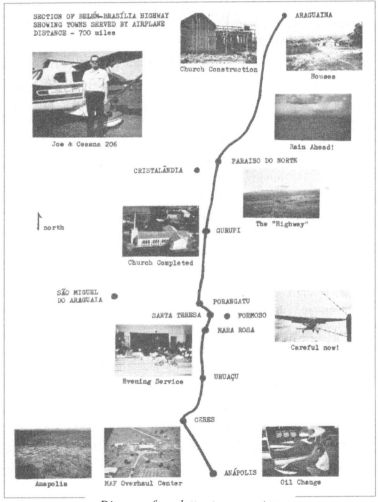

Diagram from letter to supporters

fifteen minutes to give time for the water to drain.

When I finally decided to give the landing a try, there was still what looked like an inch or so of water in the touchdown area. I put her down as slowly and gently as I could, but *whoa!* Water splashed up from the wheels high enough to cover the windshield and throw us forward against the shoulder harnesses from the rapid deceleration. It turned out okay, but if the airplane had had a tailwheel instead of a nosewheel, we would likely have been upside down hanging from our belts.

One other situation in which weather played a significant part came about after an overnight stop on the way home. I had missionary Paul Long and one of the national pastors and his wife with me. After a typical Brazilian breakfast, I was concerned that the low cloud cover had not yet lifted. Visibility looked good, so I decided to take off and circle the airstrip for a better look to help with my decision. The ceiling was only 300 or 400 feet above ground, but visibility was at least ten miles. I landed and told my passengers that we would give it a try. I expected the weather to lift soon. My plan was that if I could not proceed directly on course due to low clouds over the hills, I would turn more easterly and pick up the Belem-Brasilia highway leading to our destination of Ceres and follow it.

The weather did not cooperate by improving, and I found myself deviating more and more to the east looking for the highway I couldn't find. Not liking the situation, I decided the greater part of valor, and safety, would be to circle up through the clouds to 7,000 feet where, even though we were still flying by instrument reference only, I knew we would be well above any terrain and I could take a compass heading toward Ceres. I also had my direction finder radio (ADF) tuned in to the broadcast station in Ceres, which would lead me directly there. I figured there was a good chance the clouds would be breaking up by the time we got there and we could descend visually.

My backup plan was to use the VOR navigation radio and proceed to Brasilia for an instrument approach if necessary. I had plenty of fuel. Sure enough—and thank you, Lord—just before reaching Ceres, the clouds parted enough to allow my descent. But wait...There's more... How about a lesson learned? The lesson learned was that you can't always depend on things working out the way you planned. Fortunately, I had Plan B and C, but the radio station I used in Plan A got washed down the river a couple of weeks later in a flood.

On one trip, we had stopped at the Porto Nacional airport for fuel. While on the ground there, the national airline DC-3 arrived. This is a tailwheel type airplane. Their standard procedure was to land on the main wheels then lower the tail. About halfway through the landing, as the tail was coming down, the airplane began a swerve to the left. It left the runway, skidded across a slight gulley, which collapsed the landing gear, and looped around in a cloud of dust off to the side of the runway. No one was hurt, but the airplane looked pretty sad, not to mention the pilots.

Back in those days, world-wide, it was considered to be a critical first step after an accident to paint over the name of the airline. I'm sure it didn't take long, but we didn't hang around long enough to watch. We had things to do, places to go, and people to see.

On another trip, I noticed that the main compass suspended from the windshield and the remote compass that was mounted in the back behind the baggage compartment (with the indicator located on the instrument panel) were in disagreement with each other. The remote compass is located back there to theoretically be away from metallic things in the instrument panel area that might cause error. It was also more stable in turbulence. Which one was correct? I didn't get lost, but after getting on the ground I did some investigating. What I found was that the remote compass was in error due to the missionary's overnight bag stashed in the baggage compartment just ahead of the remote compass. It had a magnetic flashlight in it!

Speaking of navigation, the charts we had back then had several areas void of detail with lots of white space and the notation that terrain information was unknown. Flights in Brazil were often long ones of a couple of hours or more without any good landmarks—either because it was lacking on the chart or there was nothing but jungle below and no villages, rivers or mountains to help identify position. We were taught in school and pre-field training that by watching cloud shadows moving across the ground one could judge wind speed and direction at cloud level fairly well. We were also taught to read watershed direction for a general indication of the area we were in. When flying a long distance without landmarks to a destination located on a river, as was usually the case, we learned to deliberately aim several miles left or right of the destination. That way, when reaching the river if the destination was not in sight, you knew which way to turn to find it by following the river. If the aim was direct and you missed it, you'd only be guessing as to which way to turn. Another suggestion we were given for judging wind direction on the ground was to watch livestock. Cows would be tail to the wind and horses head to the wind. Not a sure thing, as you might imagine!

Navigation was a challenge during the smoke season. Each year farmers all over the country would burn their fields. Smoke would reduce the visibility down to about a mile for weeks at a time. Someone described the navigation during smoke season as trying to recognize your friend by his shoelaces.

Normally, my flights would take me way to the north toward Belem. But this day, I made a flight of an eight hour round trip flying time south to Rio de Janeiro. There was a missionary nurse in the local area that had been diagnosed with a brain tumor and needed to catch a flight from Rio back to her homeland in Europe. We loaded her in the Cessna 182, made her as comfortable as possible and, thanks to cooperative weather, delivered her safely on schedule.

MAF had closed their base in Cuiaba due to low flight demand, but would make a flight every month or two from the base in Anápolis to service the missionaries' needs there. Soon after arriving in Anápolis from language school, I was asked to go along with our Program Manager Jim Lomheim on one of these flights. We landed in Cuiabá for fuel and a load of supplies and headed for the mission station which was in Indian territory about 50 miles from the Bolivian border. Here comes culture shock number three. Upon exiting the airplane I was greeted by a sight I was no longer prepared for after buying furniture at the Sears store and riding streetcars. Men were all decked out with only G-strings and armbands. The women were naked except for a skimpy grass skirt, dirty and sitting on the ground nursing their babies. Oh, and yes, there were little round grass-roofed huts. On a different note, the small river had water clear as glass and safe to drink according to the missionary based there.

A highlight of our year at the MAF base in Anápolis was when MAF hosted a safety and training seminar. As far as I can determine, this seminar in January, 1966 was

Villagers in front of their house

the first of this kind in the missionary aviation world. Missionary pilots and mechanics from all over Brazil came for a week of classes and flying. A team of four instructors came from the USA—Hobey Lowrance of MAF, Dirk Van Dam of Moody Aviation, Terry Moose of American Airlines and Bill Kemp of American Airlines. In addition to the classroom work, each pilot received about two hours of flight instruction: an hour each of air work and takeoff/landings, and an hour of instrument training. They soon realized that the four of them were not enough to get all the flying done in time, so I was invited to become one of the flight instructors to help out. Needless to say, I felt honored to be asked.

It was a common saying that the MAF letters stood for **M**ove **A**gain **F**riend. After a year in Anápolis, we were

Missionary aviation safety seminar, Anápolis, Brazil 1966
(believed to be first ever safety seminar for aviation missions)

asked to move to the northeast coast to operate MAF's base in São Luís.

It was impractical to hire a truck to move our things due to the primitiveness of the area to be traversed. Frank and Jan Gibbs were due to furlough, so I bought their Jeep Rural (sort of like a station wagon or today's SUV). I would load what I could in the Jeep and drive there. A short-termer by the name of Noel Willems who had been helping MAF with the Piper Pacer rebuild would accompany me.

Noel was a fun guy to have around, but one day I thought he had just taken things too far. He had accompanied me on a short flight, and as I was taking off from the gravel airstrip something got my attention big time. Just as I rotated the nose up to lift off, we broke ground, but I could not get the nose of the airplane back down. The elevator control would not move, and at this angle the airplane wing would stall and we would drop to the ground. I gave a sideward glance toward Noel and he was grinning like a Cheshire cat. I thought he was messing with the controls. Afterward, I found out he was grinning because he thought I was showing off! Trying not to panic, I pushed firmly on the control wheel and all of a sudden it moved forward, the nose came down, and we resumed normal flight.

Not knowing what the problem was, I came back around and landed to check things out. What we discovered was that at the precise instant that I deflected the elevator to lift the nose, a piece of gravel had been thrown up from the left main wheel and lodged into the lead balance weight on the elevator control part of the horizontal stabilizer. It stuck there long enough that when I relaxed the control the stone became wedged between the elevator and horizontal stabilizer thus preventing the control from returning to its normal position until I had applied enough pressure to force the stone out. Years later another MAF pilot had a similar experience in Asia.

So the day came and Noel and I struck out driving to São Luís—a trip of about 1200 miles. That's a long trip over mostly narrow, non-paved roads with lots of unknowns such as places to stay, eat, and get gas. Also, there were the periodic police checkpoints. They were always suspicious of a vehicle filled to the brim with stuff. Our standard answer was, "*É mudança*," (It's a move), which seemed to satisfy them.

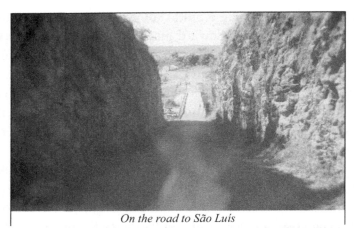

On the road to São Luís

Crossing the cattle guard bridge

Surprisingly, I don't remember much detail of the trip except the crossing of a bridge over a river during a gorgeous sunset, and an overnight stop in a tiny town of just a few buildings. There, we managed to find a "boarding house" for the night and a little something to eat. We ignored the "ladies" who seemed to want our attention.

One flat tire was the only trip problem

The only hitch of the trip I remember was one flat tire.

Noel and I returned to Anápolis where I loaded up the Piper Pacer with more stuff, including an extra plumbed-in gas tank for the extensive over-jungle portion of the flight, and flew the plane to São Luís. Frankly, I don't remember how my family, Elaine, Judy and Steve, got there. Lomheim might have taken them in the MAF Cessna, but more likely they flew on the airline.

Piper Pacer after rebuild

São Luís

We had a fairly decent house with only wooden shutters for windows. The yard had a stone wall around it about three feet high. The wall served to contain the German Shepard we inherited from the departing MAF family, Art and Marilyn McIntosh. It was only a short drive to the airport. Unlike the private MAF base in Anápolis, this airport had a control tower.

The Brazilian aviation authorities required a "*vistoria*" inspection of all aircraft every six months. Ours was due for the Pacer. I met the inspector at the agreed time at the airport, and soon it became apparent that perhaps he had imbibed a little too much alcohol over lunch. Normally I would fly, with the inspector riding along, but this guy wanted to fly the airplane himself. I inquired of his proficiency in a tailwheel type airplane, but he assured me it was no problem. Okay, I whispered to myself along with a prayer. We got in, started the engine, and began to taxi. One problem: this airplane had no communication radio, and the tower was flashing a light signal at us—one that indicated we should return to the starting point. I have no idea why unless perhaps they wanted us to use the other runway. Mr. Inspector was not happy about that, and first thing I know, he full-throttles the engine and takes off from the taxiway without tower clearance! He flies around a bit and then heads back toward the airport. Arriving in the traffic pattern and about 800 feet above the ground, the inspector reaches over and turns the ignition off and removes the key. I react by trying to turn it back on, but he gets the engine running himself and again reassures me that this is just part of the aircraft check. Crossing the runway threshold, he flares a little too high and the airplane settles in a bit hard. Trying not to sound too snide, I say something to the effect that the landing was a little firm. Again he reassures me that it's okay, it's just part of checking the airplane. He signed off on the inspection. We lived to see another day.

Two of the closest calls of my flying career came during the few months on this program. One day flying out to a village by myself, I decided to fly really low over the river. No reason, just wanted to. Remember, this was the days before operational manuals and formal standards. All of a sudden, just ahead I spied a cable across the river. Pull up! Pull up! Close call.

The second close one came when I was landing at an isolated airstrip out in the jungle. As I was about to cross the runway threshold for touchdown, another airplane zipped past a few feet above me and landed. Color my pants brown! I instantly decided the best action would be to go around and assess the situation. After a successful landing on the second try, I taxied in close to the other airplane. I didn't speak to the pilot, but I gave him the traditional Brazilian sign of rubbing the backside of my fingers up and down my cheek indicating that was a close shave.

Incidentally, in that situation, I was flying a high wing airplane and the one that passed above me was a low wing airplane. That is most often the situation with mid-air collisions of aircraft on approach to land. I couldn't see well above me and he couldn't see well below because of the wings obstructing the view.

Another incident, although not so serious, took me by surprise. My passengers were two young girls with the older one seated in the right front seat beside me. They seemed a bit nervous, but I didn't think much about it. Just as I broke ground and started the climb out, the girl in front, obviously frightened with her first airplane ride, grabbed the control wheel on her side and started yelling, "*Meu Deus, Meu Deus!*" I managed to get her hands off the control wheel, and she soon calmed down, realizing she wasn't going to die after all.

Flying the São Luís program involved taking missionaries and medical teams out for village visits rather than flying supplies to missionary outposts. The missionary I flew the most was Frank Arnold. Frank had worked in the aluminum industry in the USA before going to Brazil as a missionary. He liked community development work so took it upon himself to teach the locals how to melt scrap aluminum and recast it into pots and pans. This helped both the individuals and villages financially.

I remember one flight where I had taken Frank out for a village visit. When we had finished the work and were ready for departure, the wind had picked up somewhat but was going to be a tailwind for the takeoff. I was limited in direction of takeoff due to obstacles, and the airstrip was short. After getting the airplane into position for takeoff, we got out and literally pushed the tail back into the bushes to give us maximum runway length. Holding the brakes until the engine reached full power, we roared down the short, grass airstrip and cleared the trees without problem. Normally, I prefer a rolling turn into position for takeoff to take advantage of the momentum, but in this case the runway was too narrow to allow for that technique.

My wife, Elaine, had health issues during our time in Brazil which eventually led to the decision to return to the States to seek better care. While in language school she suffered a miscarriage followed by several D&C procedures. After moving to Anápolis these problems continued, which led to her having a hysterectomy. This was performed in the Evangelical Hospital in Anápolis. When the need for us to move to São Luís came up, it appeared that she had healed and recovered sufficiently, so we accepted the new assignment. However, shortly after arrival in São Luís she went through a period of sickness that the doctors had a hard time pinning down. At first, they said she had malaria so they started her on the treatment. However, instead of improving, she continually got worse. She lost a lot of weight. Finally, the local urologist diagnosed her with an acute case of kidney and bladder infection. Treatment came slowly since they first had to do cultures to find the right antibiotics to use. During this time the local missionaries, in observing her condition, advised us that they thought we should return to the USA for further diagnosis and treatments. Wow! Why, Lord? We've only been on this program a few months and hardly two years in country.

Communications with MAF headquarters and our Field Program Manager confirmed they were in agreement, so preparations began. This meant we had to sell most of our belongings since it was unsure when, or if, we would ever be back. We put out the word in the community and were able to sell what we needed to. We became millionaires for a day. Yep. The Jeep Rural we had bought and drove to São Luís brought in a little over a million Cruzeiros of Brazilian currency (equivalent to about US$1,200.) This took a couple of hours for our new Field Director Harold Berk and me to count, and it filled a briefcase! You see, the largest note at that time was 100 Cruzeiros, and they typically would bundle them in folded-over, rubber-banded packets of 1000 Cruzeiros. The rich feeling didn't last long because the next day we went downtown to the airline office and spent it all on our tickets to the States. Two things I especially hated to give up were my tool boxes and my cornet, which Dad had bought for me from the Bennett Blue Book mail order catalog during high school.

Before leaving the country, we were required to get approval from the government that we didn't owe any taxes. Typical of Brazil at that time, as well as many other Latin and other countries, approvals often required many visits to official departments, usually because they were looking for a little "incentive." I had made several trips into town for the approval paperwork but was always told I needed to come back since the proper person was not there to sign. What was I going to do? Our flight left in just a couple of days. I decided to try the pity party. Going back to their office, I explained, as pitifully as I knew how, about my wife being really sick and needing to find medical treatment and that our flight was soon. I threw myself at his mercy explaining that I didn't know what else to do, and that I really needed his help. It worked! By the next day I had the needed papers in hand.

We boarded our flight, overnighted in Belem courtesy of the airline, and arrived in Los Angeles the next day, where we were met by our dear MAF friends (and one of MAF's founders) the Truxtons. Thus began an entirely new phase of our lives and ministry.

I have had the privilege of going back to Brazil on several occasions to do safety seminars and/or audits, and it always excites me. When you see a place twenty, forty, or even sixty years later, the changes can be amazing. Anápolis, for example, when we lived there in the mid-1960s, had a few paved streets but most were dirt. Today, it's a bustling city with tall buildings and four-lane highways. Population has, I'm sure, at least quadrupled.

Moody Aviation alumni at Asas De Socorro (ADS) 50th Anniversary Celebration

Elaine and I had the opportunity to return for the 50th Anniversary Celebration of Asas de Socorro (ADS). ADS is the Brazilian entity that absorbed the MAF programs. ADS had long since moved their base of operations into town and was located on the Anápolis airport. The old MAF/ADS base, which had been located about seven kilometers outside of town, was forced to close due to Brazil building an air force base within a mile of it. The celebration was held at the old base property, which had been purchased by a local family. It was great to see the old base again, with all the original houses, but sad to see the old hangar turned into a cow barn. It was a fun time getting to see many of the former pilots and their families who were able to return to Brazil for the event and renew acquaintances with some Brazilians we had known earlier.

Crowd attending ADS 50th Anniversary Celebration

ADS went all out in putting on a great, God-honoring celebration. In addition to the visit to the old base, it included programs and recognitions in their new hangar facility and, of course, dinner at a Brazilian *churrascaria* (steak house.) Elaine and I were recognized as one of the pioneer families of MAF/ADS in Brazil.

Since we were going all that distance, Elaine and I decided to do some touristy stuff as well. When purchasing our airfare, we were able to add on a "Brazil Pass" which allowed us extra travel within the country for a fixed price.

We added a visit to Manaus to the north, located on the Amazon River, where we stayed with our dear friends Darrel and Lee Carver. We first met them when they came

Joe & Elaine Hopkins, Lee & Darrel Carver in Manaus

to Tennessee for Darrel to get some refresher training so he could fly the ADS Caravan float plane based in Manaus.

After the celebration, we proceeded to the Iguaçu Falls. Since the falls are located on the Brazilian border, we were able to visit both the Brazilian side and the Argentine side. Both sides have their own unique perspectives. It was a great trip, to say the least.

Elaine & Joe Hopkins at Iguacu Falls

Home Base in Fullerton, CA

After a time of getting settled in, we were living in an MAF house. At MAF's request, Elaine was seeing the mission "shrink" in case this was all in her head. (It wasn't.) She was also being checked out by doctors. I was put to work in the flight department helping Hobey Lowrance with evaluating new candidates for their flight skills and getting checked out to do some of the pre-field flight training for those going out to the field for the first time. I also did some refresher training for those returning from the field for temporary home assignments.

Since it looked like we would be there for a while, we found a house near the base to purchase with four bedrooms, one used as a den. We paid $18,500 for it. This was 1967 in Southern California. I also bought a 1964 two-door hardtop Ford Galaxy 500, green with white top. I have forgotten the price but it was well under $1,000. Gasoline was about twenty-five cents per gallon.

After about two years, we sold that house for $21,000 and bought a nicer and bigger one in Placentia for $29,000. It was less than a mile from Calvary Church, where we had become members. Pastor John Tebay and wife Grace lived about a block away around the corner. Their kids and ours were close in ages, so they became best buddies.

We made many memories there. Especially as we participated in the newly formed home "Growth Groups" the church started. Lessons learned there helped prepare us for future things ahead.

At that time, missions were trying to integrate nationals into their work, and MAF was no exception. The program administrator for the Far East had identified Ernesto as a young man in the Philippines who was interested in missionary aviation. Hank, the program admin, had flown with him in Manila and thought he had potential. Arrangements were made for him to come to Fullerton for further evaluation and training. He had very little technical experience other than driving a ramp vehicle around the airport, but he had obtained his Private Pilot license by the time he arrived in the States. Ernesto was a very soft-spoken, humble "yes, sir" kind of guy. Don Berry drew the short straw for teaching Ernesto to drive a car in Southern California. Several of us flew with Ernesto in a CE-150 we had at the time. He had some difficulty in keeping the nose of the airplane steady on the horizon, and I would occasionally remind him to watch his attitude (meaning the attitude of the aircraft nose relative to the horizon).

Years later, when Ernesto attended an International Association of Missionary Aviation (IAMA) conference, he told the group about my flying with him and telling him to watch his attitude. At the time, he thought I was telling him that he had a bad mental attitude. So much for intercultural communications! Ernesto finally did qualify to fly with MAF for a short period in Indonesia and eventually returned to the Philippines, where he started his own flying business.

Our flight orientation program involved a lot of intense, precise, close-to-the-ground type flying. It covered everything it was felt a pilot needed before being inserted into the overseas programs. Of course, there was a lot of emphasis on short field takeoffs and landings but covered other things such as package drops, airstrip evaluations, sloped runways, mountain ridge crossings and illusions, maneuvering in mountains or poor weather, navigation, and high altitude operations. This was well documented by *Plane and Pilot Magazine* in the June 1972 issue. They sent a reporter, Gene Booth, who rode with us on several flights and wrote the story. My trainee for those flights was Jim Lynne, who was preparing for service in West Irian (later called Irian Jaya, and now Papua). The writer was especially impressed with our package drop demo. Here is how he described it in the magazine article:

Wingspan, by the book, for the Cessna 180 is 36.2 feet. That final two-tenths of a foot seems mighty big at this moment. Our red and white workhorse is committed to a full flap approach, ticking over with slight power, through a narrow V-shaped notch slashing a gap in the mountain ridge, towards a canyon valley just beyond. As the wingtips swish past the scrub brush inches away on each side, the pilot dumps half the flaps to increase the 180's sink to the absurdly narrow valley floor, a long cliff-drop below. From judgement and long experience, he casually adds power to stop the sink and holds the airplane in slow flight 100 feet above the gully below, sloping downhill away from us. The 12-foot round stock watering tank, our "target" for this simulated package drop, slips past the left wing below. And dead ahead is a sheer wall of granite, where the capricious gully-floor veers at a sharp right angle to the left. Even for the 180 wonderplane, and even had it been lightly loaded, a climb-out straight ahead is impossible. Up on the left wingtip, still at half flap but with full power now (and no apparent increase in rump pressure on seat cushion), the bird bends around to follow the canyon. As the pilot levels off and climbs past the canyon opening to the broad valley beyond, the rest of the flaps are hauled in, and normal best rate-of-climb speed is selected. "Have to be careful there," Joe Hopkins tells his student in the left seat and this suddenly stiffened passenger behind. "The wind is off the ocean today, and it could cause a bad downdraft right at that opening ridge," he continues. ...This trip through the gap has been our fourth circuit, each one progressively lower as the pilot gets the lay of the land and feels out the approach and package drop problem. As tight and puckerish as it has been, it still was not quite the proper technique. There is a little too much turbulence, so Joe keeps a margin of speed and altitude in hand for the demonstration. Or so he says. In the left seat, Jim Lynne is a former U.S. Navy pilot from Pensacola. But he is a student pilot here, and he is sweating from the exertions common to that long-suffering period of cram and prod. The vertical scenery we are playing wingtip tag with helps not a whit. "Still want to be a bush pilot?" I wondered aloud, to relieve my own tensions as much as anything. "Yeah, I think so," Jim smiled.

One day while heading out of the Los Angeles basin to our practice area, I had the trainee under the hood for a few minutes of instrument practice. He said, "Was that an airplane I heard?" just as I glanced out the right side window in time to see a twin-engine Aero Commander crossing directly below us. When the airplane is close enough to hear its engines, it is too close!

Occasionally, I would fly an MAF airplane from Fullerton to the Los Angeles International Airport to pick up or deliver a passenger who had arrived via the airlines. Incredible as it seems today, I would land and taxi to one of the airline terminal buildings, call ground control and get a gate assignment to park my little airplane. Usually, I shut down and went inside the terminal through the loading/unloading gate to find my passenger. Just for fun, with the passenger loaded and ready to go, I would sometimes call ground control, give him my gate number and tell him, "Cessna Nxxxxx ready for push back."

We had permission to practice on several dirt airstrips in the area. But one we did not have permission to use one that belonged to Art Scholl, a popular aerobatic pilot at the time. However, we would sometimes use his airstrip to simulate forced landings or to do low passes to practice a runway evaluation—but without landing.

My trainee and I were flying a Cessna 172 on a particular day. It had electrically operated wing flaps. Overhead the airstrip, I closed the throttle and asked the trainee to simulate a forced landing.

He did a good job, so on final approach I told him I now wanted him to change to a low pass over the airstrip for a simulated runway evaluation. As we progressed along the runway I noticed that the airplane was losing airspeed, and we were now just a few feet above the runway. I asked him to check to make sure the wing flaps were retracted to 20 degrees. Nope! They were still extended fully at 40 degrees. Frantically looking around, I noticed that the flap circuit breaker had popped. Quickly resetting the breaker, we managed to get the flaps up to 20 degrees. But the airplane still was not performing well, and we were running out of runway and airspeed. The stall warning horn began to beep. I then noticed that the trainee had forgotten to turn off the carburetor heat after the simulated forced landing, and this was robbing us of some power.

Immediately correcting that issue, we eked out a bit more power. We crossed the far threshold of the runway and were over a small canyon dip but approaching a ridge. There we were—airspeed was near the bottom peg, nose up and struggling, stall horn blaring, and a slight ridge ahead. If only we could clear that ridge, we could then make a turn downhill toward the valley. The wheels of the airplane rolled ever so lightly across the top of the ridge, which fortunately had no vegetation, and we started the turn. Whew. Free to fly another day. Thank you, Lord. Lesson learned: Don't try to combine training items on the fly. Plan and prepare for each one as a separate project.

Independent Medical Mission was a group of doctors, dentists and other medical personnel based in Southern California that was doing medical mission trips to Mexico. Several of them were pilots, mostly at the

Private Pilot level, and flew their own planes. They decided they would like to have MAF along with them for the "professional" influence. MAF agreed this was something we could help with since we would be taking a trainee or two along and it would be an excellent opportunity for training and exposure. One of their group lived in Tucson and would fly down to the mountain area near Chihuahua ahead of time to get things set up. Typically, our group would leave California on Thursday and fly to Tucson where we would overnight and get ready for an early morning departure into Mexico. This was an excellent stopover because the Ron-Tel (a play on words, RON is pilot speak for Remain Over Night) was located right on the airport next to the control tower. There was also a restaurant. Land, taxi in, unload, and walk right in to the motel. How convenient is that! The area we would fly to for the clinics was located on a plateau area in the mountains at about 7,000 feet elevation. A couple of dirt airstrips served the several villages there. Clinics would be held on Friday and Saturday with a return to California on Sunday.

One of the pilots was flying his own plane, which was a Mooney. He told the story of flying into an airstrip with a passenger. The passenger was a missionary working in the area and had been around for many years. He knew influential people including the governor. And he liked to talk. The airstrip required that the pilot sort of slide down one slope on the approach and then flare uphill onto the airstrip. It required concentration. As he tells it, he was sweating it out, concentrating on the approach when all of a sudden the missionary slapped him on the back and yelled over the engine noise, "Say, did I tell you what the governor said?" So much for sterile cockpit procedures!

To illustrate the skill level of some of the pilots in the group, there was this one trip where the pilot had brought his daughter along in his own plane. When we left for the return to the States and arrived in Tucson after having to work around some weather, this pilot and his plane didn't show up. We learned later that his navigation skills were not so great. When confronted with the weather, he just kept going further east where it looked better and eventually ended up somewhere in New Mexico.

Short Field Takeoff and Landing (STOL) airplane modifications were becoming popular in the late 60s and 70s, some of which were the Wren, the Robinson, the Owl, and the Horton. MAF had a Cessna 180 in southern Mexico with the Robinson kit installed. In California we had a 180 modified that we were evaluating with the Owl which was less complex and cheaper. In doing takeoff and landing tests at the Corona airport, which was near sea level, it was hard to determine which was best because the differences were so small and pilot technique might account for a lot of it. It was decided that Hobey Lowrance and I would fly the one modified with the Owl down to the MAF base in Mitla, Mexico where Milt Anderson was based. He was using short mountain airstrips that were several thousand feet up in elevation. With the reduced engine performance at altitude, perhaps we could better compare performances. Milt had flown the standard un-modified Cessna 180 and was now using the Robinson modified version. He should be able to judge and compare much more easily. What we found was that the Owl would get off the ground almost as soon as the Robinson but would then hesitate before a good climb was established. On the other hand, the Robinson would get off and then go right on into the climb. This would matter mostly in situations where you had an immediate low obstacle such as bushes or corn right after liftoff.

Hobey and I alternated flying legs on the trip down and back home. On the way back we were discussing fuel stops and, not wanting to take more time than necessary, decided we could make it all the way to Hermosillo. The plan was to run one wing tank completely dry so we would have maximum fuel in the other tank for landing. When the engine quit, Hobey lifted the wing in order to get the last few drops out of that tank before switching. After landing and refueling we could tell by the looks on the face of the line attendant that he knew we only had a couple of gallons left. Lesson learned. But, hey, this was before the days of Operations Manuals and written company standards. Maybe we should have studied the Bible more carefully and learned from the Israelites when they had no kings or judges and every man did what was right in his own eyes.

Jack Walker was to fly a Cessna from California down to the MAF base in San Cristobal de Las Casas in the southern tip of Mexico, and for some reason I and Ray Morgret, the MAF radio technician, were going with him. It was a fun trip. We overnighted in Zihuatanejo and stayed in a quaint hotel right on the beach. The water was nice for an evening swim, which surprised me because the Pacific Ocean in southern California was cold enough in July and August to freeze your toes off. We continued our journey and stopped at the MAF base in Mitla for a visit with the family there and drop off a few things. The last leg between Mitla and Las Casas became quite interesting. Meandering around between cloud buildups, we noticed that the airplane was rising, as verified by the winding altimeter and significant rate of climb shown on the vertical speed indicator. All of a sudden the bottom dropped out and, like the astronauts, we experienced zero gravity except even more so. Water came out of our drinking cups and cookie crumbs floated before our faces. Wow, just as soon not do that again!

Some Mexico airstrips were quite challenging

It was great being with the Walkers in Las Casas. That was the jumping off place for flights down to the Summer Institute of Linguistics (SIL) Jungle Camp base. Jack took me on a tour of not only Jungle Camp, but also to several other airstrips he was using. Some were very challenging. He would fly into a strip first, then let me try some of them. We didn't have to switch seats since I was as comfortable in the right seat as the left. One I remember could have turned out badly but fortunately didn't. The surface had some bounders and I caught one the wrong way and got into quite an oscillating bounce routine before getting things under control again.

After being back at MAF headquarters for a couple of years and Elaine's health doing quite well, we were asked to go back to Brazil short term to fill a need in the Boa Vista program in northern Brazil. We were excited about the opportunity, so we loaded up the family and did a cross-country sweep visiting our supporters with the plan to end up with my parents in North Carolina before getting our flight to Brazil. Like we used to say about the weather in Chicago, "If you don't like the weather, just wait a minute." Upon arrival at my parents in NC, we received a call from MAF saying that plans had changed and that we should return to California. Dang!

We needed transport for the family back to California and there was a big, black Cadillac with tail fins for sale for $300. It had a crunched right fender but was drivable. The purchase was completed, and we were on our way. Great trip, with the only down side being the 8 miles per gallon of fuel consumption! Still, the trip was much cheaper than airfare for our family of four. Arriving back in California, I kept the car and had one of the new MAF orientees with body repair experience fix the fender. I got lots of ribbing over driving a big, black Cadillac even though I had paid much less for it than for the Ford Galaxy 500. I wasn't alone in the Cadillac club at MAF. Norm

Olsen also had one of the same vintage except that his was yellow.

In 1967, I was asked to fly a new Cessna 180, which had been purchased by the Methodist Church, to New Orleans where it would be shipped overseas. First, I was to fly it to Charlotte, NC where the mission had scheduled a dedication service. As reported in their news release, "The $20,000 Cessna 180 is part of a $100,000 memorial undertaken this year by the Western North Carolina Conference in honor of the late Dr. George Way Hartley, medical missionary to Liberia...The airplane is being flown here from California by Joe Hopkins, a member of Missionary Aviation Fellowship and a native of North Carolina. The aircraft will then be flown to New Orleans, packed and shipped to Liberia for missions work in the nation where Dr. Harley spent a lifetime, establishing a major medical center at Ganta and five jungle clinics." The dedication service was held at gate 8 at the Charlotte airport.

My mom felt the need for a visit to California to see her grandkids. My old home town (now called Eden after the name change from Draper) was not far out of the way, so I arranged to pick her up. She could fly back to California with me by way of Charlotte and New Orleans. After dropping off the airplane in New Orleans, we would take the airline to Wichita, where I was to pick up another new Cessna and fly it back to California. Not being accustomed to flying in small planes, she loaded up with a supply of Dramamine for the trip—thinking it was worth all kinds of hardships to see the grandkids. By the second day she ditched the Dramamine, saying she was missing too much. It was quite an adventure for her, and she really enjoyed our journey across the country together.

Wanting another child, we looked into adoption through the county. After jumping through all the paperwork hoops, we were advised of a new-born baby girl becoming available. We visited her to get acquainted and felt she was the one for us. Thus we welcomed Christy Lynn into the family—our California sunshine. Before we took delivery, unbeknownst to us until after the fact, she had a surgical procedure for pyloric stenosis—with no further aftereffects. A few months later, one of her eyes became slightly crossed, so we arranged for corrective surgery. This went well. However, she did require one more surgery after we moved to Tennessee to completely correct the problem. She has been amazingly healthy since then and, to date, continues to be a delightful special blessing to us, along with our other two children.

Honduras Interlude

Another opportunity for short term service arose. (Remember, it was said that MAF meant Move Again Friend.)There was a pilot shortage in Honduras due to furloughs, and we agreed to go fill the need. This time, with the addition of Christy to the family, we had three kids in tow.

We flew commercial into San Pedro Sula on the north coast of Honduras where we were met by Paul Weir, MAF pilot and Program Manager. Loading our whole family and our luggage into the Cessna 180 for the anticipated five month stay, we made the 30 minute flight

Hopkins family in Honduras 1970

to Siguatepeque, which would be our new home. Siguat, which we called it for short, was located at an elevation of about 3,500 feet above sea level just north of the Comayagua valley and about a 30 minute flight north of the capitol of Tegucigalpa.

The base had a hangar, grass runway, and four MAF couples besides ourselves living there—one husband was a dentist, one was a radio technician, and the other two were pilots. Aircraft based at Siguatepeque consisted of two Cessna 180's with Robertson STOL conversions and a Piper Pacer. Typical flights were only 20 to 30 minutes long and were mostly air ambulance flights. Even though Honduras was a poor third-world country, it had a fairly good telegraph system. When villages around the country had a medical emergency, they would send us a telegram asking for the airplane. This meant that we never knew from day to day what flying we would have until the telegrams came in. There was an evangelical hospital in Siguatepeque. We gave the patients the choice of being

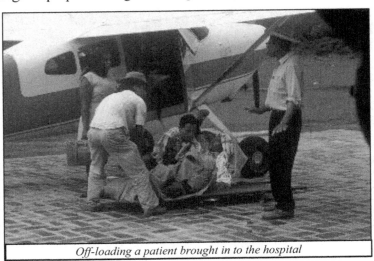

Off-loading a patient brought in to the hospital

Nurses in training on Honduras

brought there or us taking them to Tegucigalpa to the public hospital. Most chose the evangelical hospital, which justified our providing the service. The hospital had a chaplain who ministered to the patients while in the hospital and often followed up with a visit to their village after they returned home.

We always carried a box of gospel tracts in the airplane and gave them out to those who gathered around the airplane when we landed. With hardly any exceptions, the tracts were enthusiastically received.

We distributed gospel tracts at every opportunity

It didn't take a lot of field checkout for me upon arrival, since I had been doing the flight orientation training for a couple of years at headquarters. Mostly, I just needed to learn the airstrips. Honduras had some of the shortest and most primitive airstrips of any of the MAF programs worldwide. Most of these had no missionary based there to maintain the runway but rather belonged to the local village. We always had to be on the lookout for temporary rock markers and goal posts the locals left on the airstrip after their soccer game—not to mention the cows, horses and pigs. Many had ill-defined borders, slope, rough spots, drop-offs at the approach or far end or both.

And there were thorns. We tried to keep them off of the airstrip and avoided taxiing where they might be, but occasionally a thorn would, unknowingly, pierce the airplane tire. We might not know it for several days until the slow leak finally resulted in a flat tire.

Some airstrips were as short as 600-700 feet long. That's why the STOL Cessna was needed. Also, we generally limited our loads to half a tank of gas, the patient and one accompanying person. Paul Weir, the Program Manager, did not have a flight instructor license, so his procedure for new pilot checkouts was to fly the plane himself into an airstrip explaining the procedure as he went. He would then get out and have the new pilot do a couple of takeoffs and landings on his own before going to the next location. I kept a little notebook with me where I wrote down pertinent information about each airstrip I went into, including a rough diagram of runway slope profile. I had about 60 airstrips in my notebook by the end of my five months there.

The kids always enjoyed the sugar cane

Judy and Steve attended the local mission school, and all three kids enjoyed the tropical birds, freedom to wander around, playing with the other MAF kids, and sucking on sugar cane.

Three special events related to my flying experience there stand out.

The first one involved a short flight I made in the Piper Pacer. I dropped off a public works passenger at a little airstrip called Conception, after which I was going about five minutes away to another airstrip, Magdalena, and then return to the first one to pick up the worker going back to Siguatepeque. The first airstrip had a slight slope, and we usually landed uphill. When I arrived, I noticed workmen were doing some construction on the small hillside at the upper end. When I returned to pick up my passenger for the flight back home, I decided I would make a straight-in approach and land downhill since the airplane was light with no load. Everything was looking good on the approach until about a quarter of a mile out I noticed what looked like a huge cloud of dust at the top end of the airstrip. Whoa! What was that? I decided I had better abort

Airstrip under construction shortly before the dynamite incident described

the landing and check things out. Passing by the side of the airstrip, I didn't see anything that looked out of the ordinary, so I continued with an approach to land uphill. After touching down and coming to a stop one of the workers came breathlessly running over to the airplane and said, "Another five seconds and you would have been with God!" They had not seen me coming until after lighting the fuse on dynamite they had set in the side of the hill at the upper end of the airstrip. It had gone off just as I was about to land and accounted for the huge dust cloud I had seen.

The second event started as I was helping Paul get ready for his afternoon flight to take a patient from the hospital back home. Destination was a small airstrip right on the border with San Salvador. As he got seated, he asked me if I wanted to go along to further my orientation to the area. "Sure," I said as I jumped in the right front seat. It was only about a half hour flight each way. We would be back soon. Not! We landed and got the recovered patient on his way. There was an armed soldier there at the airstrip, but that was nothing out of the ordinary as far as we were concerned. Relations between Honduras and Salvador had been tense for some time. However, as we started to get back in the airplane, the soldier came over and said he could not let us go until he got approval from the comandante in town. Paul said we would wait. We waited and waited.

Finally, Paul decided he had better go into town and see what was taking so long. I would stay with the airplane. About an hour later someone else arrives with a horse and says I should come into town, also. Uh-Oh! What now? Securing the airplane, I went with him. Well, the word was that an order had been issued saying that no airplanes were allowed to land at that airstrip—and especially the evangelical airplane. It would surely have been nice if they had told us beforehand. The comandante already knew Paul and was very apologetic. Word got out in town, and the local Christians went to bat for us by providing a place to sleep and inviting us for meals while we were under house arrest. I enjoyed a cup of hot cinnamon tea. They even shared toothpaste and toothbrushes that had been left there earlier by missionaries.

The next day came and went with still no approval. We had been able to call back to home base via the airplane's radio to report our situation, but they didn't know what to believe. Were we under duress in reporting that things were okay? They didn't know. We saw the other MAF plane circling in the distance to verify that things looked alright. That evening Paul, who was a real evangelist at heart, arranged to have a street meeting in the village square. Who knows, perhaps we'll meet someone in heaven as a result of that gathering? When life serves you lemons, make evangelical lemonade, right? Finally, the next morning—after two nights there—brought word that we were free to leave. A hug, shower, and shave were very welcome upon arrival home.

The third event was a fun one. The town of Siquatepeque had a Christmas tradition that MAF helped with. We brought Santa Claus to town. The town Santa would sneak into our hangar and get into the airplane while the hangar doors were closed. We then opened the doors, rolled out the airplane and taxied out for takeoff. By then, practically the whole town, knowing what was going to happen, had gathered at the airstrip. I was the privileged pilot, so I took off, briefly circled around out of sight, and

Santa Claus after arrival via MAF airplane

The crowd storming the airstrip to see Santa

then came back in for the landing. I had to roll out long and shut down quickly since the crowd was running after the airplane knowing that Santa had arrived. Santa dismounted from the airplane to the cheers of the crowd and got into the back of a pickup truck where he proceeded to throw candy to everyone.

We left Honduras about the middle of January, 1971, and returned to the States by way of NC to celebrate a delayed Christmas with my family there. Sadly, about two weeks after we left, Paul Weir, the Program Manager, was killed in a plane crash along with his two passengers when the plane hit a mountain just a few miles from the Siguatepeque base. That event, along with another MAF fatal crash soon after in California, set the stage for my beginning involvement in missionary aviation safety.

Joe counting pills in the clinic during mission trip

Forty-four years later, in 2015, daughter Christy and I had the privilege of returning to Honduras for a week. We were part of a mission trip from our church. A team of eight of us spent a week just outside of Comayagua at the *El Ayudante* (The Helper) mission base, helping them with their community outreach ministry. They have a really nice medical clinic with doctors and nurses, in addition to providing dental and eye care. All patients who go through the clinic are provided with spiritual counseling and a Bible if they don't have one. They come from miles around, mostly walking. Typically, there will be dozens lined up early in the morning waiting to receive medical attention.

In addition to helping at the clinic, we participated in Vacation Bible Schools, local church services, building outside toilets, pouring cement floors, painting the local school building and installing/servicing water filters. The main community water source is a canal running through the village. It is used for washing clothes, bathing, and even drinking water. The water filters are amazing and consist of simply a large plastic container into which is placed a layer of large stones, then a layer of smaller stones, and then covered with a special sand. Even the dirtiest water can be poured into the top and after it makes its way through the sand and stones, emerges as pure drinking water. The filters have been a major boost for the health of the community.

On the way from the San Pedro Sula airport to *El Ayudante*, we passed through Siguatepeque and, with the help of Google Maps, found the house we previously had lived in. The old MAF housing looked much different, and the airstrip we used had been closed. Nevertheless, it brought back many pleasant memories.

As I write this, I am preparing to leave for another mission trip to Honduras—six years after the one described above. The group from my church will be going back to the same place, as they do each year.

Back in California

Moving back into our house in Placentia, CA, after our five-month stint in Honduras, I settled in once again to doing MAF pre-field flight training, evaluation of new candidates, and refresher flying for MAFers returning from the field for furlough. By this time, Hobey Lowrance had moved into other responsibilities and I was given the title of Manager of Technical Training. Before this time, I had worked with Ernie Krenzin, who since had left MAF. Now, my colleagues helping with the flight training were Bob Johansen and John Gettman. Soon, one of MAF's first pilots, Hatch Hatcher, who with wife Penny served many years in Mexico, returned from the field and also helped some. Since most of his career had been as a field pilot he was not as comfortable in his role as trainer but actually adjusted very well.

It was a nice Southern California day and Elaine was at home listening to the Christian radio station. Suddenly, there was an announcement on the air that an MAF airplane had crashed with no survivors. She, paralyzed with fear, just knew it had to be me since she didn't think any of the other instructors were on duty that day. Hoping that word would come by way of a visit rather than a phone call, the phone rang. It was Jim Lomheim calling from the office to let her know of the crash and that

I was not involved. In fact, Tom Albright and I were already on our way driving to the crash site located on a ridge just south of the Corona Pass. Arriving on site, the FAA investigator allowed us to survey the smoldering wreckage lying on a steep slope. One wing was flat on the ground with the charred remains of the cabin portion of the fuselage lying on top. The other wing was detached and about 100 feet down the hill. The engine only burrowed into the hillside a few inches due to the hardness of the surface. It was obvious the airplane had impacted the ground perpendicular to the surface and immediately burst into flames. Hatch Hatcher was the MAF instructor and the "student" was an airline pilot who was on a stopover in Los Angeles and interested in possibly serving with MAF. Hatch was giving him an introductory evaluation flight.

After the accident in Honduras a few months earlier, David Hall contacted MAF. David was a friend of one of the passengers killed in the Honduras accident. David was also an instructor at the University of Southern California where he taught in the Aircraft Accident Investigation and Prevention Course. He offered to help in any way he could, but MAF didn't appear interested in his help. Now, after this second fatal accident, David again came knocking at MAF's door and insisted on being of service. He offered to get a slot in the USC course for someone from MAF. There would be little or no cost since USC had met their quota for the course and graciously made the offer at David's request. Charlie Mellis, MAF's president at the time, asked me if I would consider becoming MAF's safety officer and taking the two week course.

The course was thorough and enlightening. It included wreckage analysis, human factors, aerodynamics, photography and other pertinent information needed to find the cause of an accident and come up with recommendations for prevention of other accidents from happening. Putting my newly acquired knowledge and training to work, I did a retroactive investigation of this accident, the earlier one in Honduras, and several others. I wrote reports of them and distributed them to MAF personnel. I also began an MAF in-house publication called *The Subject is Safety*, in which I wrote safety articles with the goal of preventing future accidents. We did research on aircraft crashworthiness, fire prevention, decision making, etc. We also looked into the use of helmets for our pilots. We experimented in wearing various models of motorcycle helmets during our flight training. Objections began coming in from our pilots like, "They are too hot to wear in the tropics." "What will our passengers think if the pilot wears a helmet? Especially, if we don't offer them to passengers, as well." Ad nauseam.

By wearing them in the 100 degree heat of southern California and setting an example, we tried to win them over. We found a Christian guy in the local area who had an interest in missions and also had a company that made custom fit helmets. I got fitted for the first one. They used a clay-type heated molding material over your head to get the dimensions and used that to make the helmet liner. I went to pick it up when it was finished and, boy, it felt two sizes too small! I decided to wear it home during my drive from the office to see if I could get used to it. Imagine this, a guy wearing a helmet, driving a big black Cadillac through downtown Fullerton! While stopped at a stoplight, a car with two young guys pulled up beside me in the inside lane, rolled down the window and inquired, "Hey, what's happening, man?" I soon got used to the tight-fit feeling, and we began getting other MAF pilots fitted. We paid $65 for the first ones. That was without a visor or earpieces and microphone—but it did come with my name on the back!

I wrote an article, *The Subject is Safety,* which was published in the MAF *Mission Aviation* constituency newsletter. It was the May-June 1972 issue. Below is a summary:

After 23 years with no fatalities, now six accidents claiming 16 lives over five years

MAF pilots are human. God has not promised that missionaries (or any of His other children) are exempt from failure, accidents, and suffering. We have a responsibility to do the best we can with the knowledge and abilities He has given us.

MAF operated for twenty-three years without a fatality. We praise the Lord for this. But, suddenly, within the past five years, six fatal accidents have claimed sixteen lives. It is true that we now fly more miles in a month than we averaged per year during our first thirteen years. But even the sky-rocketing increase in exposure due to more hours flown does not justify the accidents.

We are concerned.

For the past several years we have been increasing our efforts in accident prevention. Two years ago our Research Director, Chuck Bennett, conducted a disciplined analysis of all aircraft accidents and near accidents by Protestant mission pilots since 1946. The purpose of the study was to find the most frequent kinds of accidents, and their causes. Survey forms were sent to 250 mission pilots. Some 85,000 bits of information were categorized and cross-correlated by computer. Last year he conducted a still more intensive investigation of every accident or near accident of any kind since 1963 in which any American MAF pilot was involved. The resultant fifty page report was the subject of intense scrutiny by every MAF pilot. A number of changes have taken place as a result of these studies. Perhaps the most significant is a new systematic program of on-the-field flight training and evaluation for all MAF pilots. We have tightened our screening of new pilots and increased the length of their field check-out period significantly. We are doing research and development in the areas of better engine reliability, crash helmets, stronger aircraft cabins, and fire prevention. We are evaluating different types of aircraft such as the Helio Courier and twin engine airplanes from the standpoint of both safety and utility. The MAF Board of Directors has made aviation safety one of its **formal goals**. Pilots are encouraged to share their "close calls" in greater depth for the benefit of others. They are required to fill out a detailed questionnaire after any accident. This helps us evaluate the causes of accidents and in turn prevent future occurrences by altering procedures or modifying our equipment. Two of us have attended a special course at the University of

Southern California on aircraft accident investigation and prevention. This helped us see how the various causes of accidents manifest themselves, such as mechanical failures and physical and psychological problems. The factors we've discussed here—pilot training, accident reporting and investigation, research, the influence of professionals from outside MAF—will, we trust, help us reach our goal. As we bend every effort toward safety in a responsible manner, we are fully committed to the sovereignty of the will of our Lord. In His hands we are fully safe, accidents or no accidents.

Each year Moody Aviation would bring their flight students to the MAF headquarters for a visit as part of their Advanced Cross-Country (AXC) training. The Moody staff was meeting with the MAF staff administration. At the last minute I was invited to sit in. During the meeting, Dirk Van Dam spoke of the desire to have another flight instructor join the Moody staff—one that had field experience. The feeling was that students had a special respect for one who had "been there, done that." Somehow, that got my attention, and it seemed the Holy Spirit was prompting me to pursue the idea. I broached the idea with my MAF boss Tom Albright and also Van Dam telling them that I felt I should at least pursue the idea and see where it leads. My wife and I discussed it, and she was open to the idea—bless her heart, she always supported me in decisions regarding our future. I took out paper and pen and began to jot down the pros and cons of making the change. The cons won out—on paper. I should stay with

MAF. But I could never get away from the fact that the prompting seemed to come from the Lord that I should make the change. So that's what I based my decision on for the move to a new phase in my life in Tennessee. I found out later at Moody that the strong feeling that the Lord had called me there was the thing that would keep me there through some very tough times.

I already felt an affinity with Moody since for two years during the month of May, Dirk had me go out to Tennessee for two weeks and fly with each of the graduating students and give them a large chunk of their "tactical" flight training. As a special blessing, during one of those two-week stints, Moody provided an instructor and use of their Twin Comanche to get my multiengine rating.

Moody sent a moving van to transport our stuff from California to Tennessee. They also provided their Cessna 210 for me to fly my family there. MAFers Don and Phyllis Berry needed a car to drive to the east coast during part of their deputation, so they drove my Ford Galaxy 500 and delivered it to me when finished. I sold the big black Cadillac before leaving California.

Moody Aviation in Tennessee

We made the move in June of 1972.

We found a house to buy in the Stoney Creek area about two miles from the Elizabethton airport. It was on a triangular piece of property surrounded on two sides by Stoney Creek, where it split. From the main highway one had to cross a narrow wooden bridge. When the moving van arrived, the drivers took one look at the bridge and decided there was no way they would cross it. They went around through a subdivision and came to our house the back way across the other branch of the creek, which had two large steel culverts and was covered over with dirt. No problem. But it's a good thing they came when they did, because several weeks later a huge rain storm came, the creek flooded big time, and the culverts were washed away, leaving our only access to be the wooden bridge.

We looked for a church home but became "church tramps" for quite a while before finding one we felt like joining. After several years in that church, we joined another. After several more years another opportunity arose. Dr. Charles Shepson, of the Christian and Missionary Alliance (C&MA), had moved to Elizabethton and started a Christian retreat center. He wanted to see a C&MA church in Elizabethton and called a meeting of any who might be interested. Somehow we heard about it and attended the meeting. One thing led to another, and a small group started meeting in our house on Thursday evenings to see what might become of it. Long story short, out of that group the Elizabethton Alliance Church was formed. We were proud to be charter members. I served on the Governing/Elder board and Elaine got the nursery developed in addition to serving as head deaconess and in other roles. The Lord blessed, and the church attendance grew to about 150 with a thriving youth group.

Elaine got a job as school nurse for the Elizabethton City Schools. She really enjoyed that job and made lots of friends as she visited a different school each day. The thing she didn't like was the commute into town for her job. Our kids were not too happy about their time in the county schools either. Two years later we found a house we liked in the city, but it was not for sale. The widow living there was not ready to move. We told her we were interested and to let us know if she decided to sell. Not too long after that, she called. We made the move on March 24, 1974, Christy's birthday. We paid $29,000 for the Stoney Creek house, sold it for slightly more, and bought the house in the city for $31,500. By the time we sold it in 2015, we had bought the back lot behind it and also added a 650 sq. ft. addition to the house. The addition was paid for by proceeds from an investment in hotel properties we had made while still living in California. (This investment had been made available to MAFers by a Christian businessman.) There were many more improvements to the house over the years, including carpeting, kitchen remodel, central heat and air, and adding a carport. After living there for over 40 years, we sold the house for $165,000, which was well below what it was worth. Potential buyers were unnecessarily concerned about the asbestos roof and what it would cost to replace it. They need not have been concerned. The roof had been in place since it was built in 1941 and still had many more years of life in it.

I jumped right into my job at Moody Aviation and

got my baptism by fire. The schedule demands were great. After the week of flight camp in the summer when we flew with and evaluated applicants for the course, we began flight training for those who were accepted. At the end of the summer, these students went into full time A&P mechanics training for a year. But in addition to their maintenance training eight hours per day, they were expected to continue their flight training before school in the mornings and after school plus Saturdays. Guess who gave them their flight training. Right! The flight instructors, in addition to flying with their advanced flight students, were also required to fly with the maintenance students before and after regular school hours and on Saturdays.

But wait. There's more. Moody was also providing air taxi services to the community including the local funeral home in transporting bodies. So we were assigned about one weekend per month to be on call for any flights that came up. Often we were able to take students along with us on these flights for the exposure. I remember one flight when we left in the evening and went way up north somewhere and didn't get back home until about 3:00 A.M. We were still expected to show up the next morning at eight for our regular day. There was little time left for the family. This is why I mentioned earlier that I felt the only thing that kept me there during all this was the sense of the Lord's calling I had when I left MAF. Eventually, after several years of that, the program was rearranged, and the air taxi commitment was dropped, so some of the pressure was relieved.

One of my early air taxi (ATCO) flights involved flying the Cessna 206 to Portsmouth, VA on a Saturday to pick up a body for the funeral home. At about the same time the hearse pulled up with the body and we got it loaded into the airplane, a man got out of a vehicle, came over to the plane and identified himself as being with the FAA. He wanted to see my air taxi permit. Of course, Moody had proper licensing for ATCO work, but for some reason I did not have the personal paperwork yet showing me as being an approved ATCO pilot. I called Dirk Van Dam to see what I should do. He contacted our FAA office in Nashville and verified that, indeed, I did need a permit. The local FAA guy that stopped me said that, so far, I had not broken any rules because I was still on the ground. He said I could either off-load the body and go back home or get someone else to make the flight that was approved. After communicating this to Dirk, he got another Moody pilot, who was approved, and flew another plane down to Portsmouth. I rode back to Elizabethton with Dirk and the other pilot flew the body back.

One of the highlights of the Moody training for the students in their final year of training was the advanced cross-country trip (AXC). This was a two week trip, using six to eight airplanes, in which the students would get to experience flying all the way down from Tennessee into southern Mexico and to California. Each airplane typically had an instructor and two or three students. We went in two groups. One group would fly the taildragger Cessna 185s and the nosewheel 206 and take the southern route across the USA to Brownsville, TX, where they would enter Mexico. The other group would fly the retractable gear Cessna 210s and Bonanza A-36s and go, more-or-less, across the mid-section of the USA. They would make a point of flying into the large airports such as Memphis, Denver, El Paso, and Phoenix for the experience that would offer. They would end up at the MAF headquarters in California. The southern group would typically use the smaller airports in Mexico and visit several mission bases with a route that would usually include places such as Veracruz on the gulf coast, Mexico City, mission bases in Mitla and San Cristobel de Las Casas, then back up the Pacific western coast with stops along the way such as Puerto Vallarta and Mazatlán, ending up at the MAF headquarters. More often than not, they would have the opportunity to see and fly into some of the very airstrips used by the missions in Mexico. After a short visit with MAF, the students switched airplanes, and those who flew through Mexico would return across the USA in the retractables, and vice versa. This was very valuable training and contributed greatly to their flight experience and development into mature pilots.

Although my instructing time at Moody did involve some tight, precision flying during the tactical training such as canyon turns, mountain flying, and package drops, I never had any close calls during that time. I recall one situation, however, that may deserve a few lines of narrative. My student and I had just taken off and were heading to the practice area in a Cessna 172. Arriving at the desired altitude, the student retarded the throttle to level off, but there was no power reduction. The engine remained at full climb power. Hmmm, this was interesting.

Seeing that we had no throttle control, we notified the dispatcher by radio and headed back to the airport. My plan was that we would continue climbing on the way back in order to have plenty of altitude over the airport. Then we would cut the power with the mixture control and make a power-off gliding approach to the landing. This would require judicious control of the approach path, but hey, this is why we practice simulated forced landings, right?

Positioning ourselves on a high downwind leg, we cut the power with the mixture control and began the glide. The student was still in control, and I only had to give minimal coaching. With four thousand feet of runway available, we decided to plan the touchdown at mid-field, which would give us a thousand feet of runway to get slowed and still have enough energy to take the next exit (1000 feet from the far end of the runway) and clear the runway before coasting to a stop. And that's the way it was. Touchdown was right on the money, and we coasted to a stop just clear of the runway. Just another day at the office!

Oh, the problem, you ask? A maintenance issue during the last inspection. The throttle cable was not properly secured and had detached from the throttle arm at the carburetor. Fortunately, the design allowed for the throttle to remain at full power rather than going to idle.

Not too long after moving to Tennessee, MAF asked me to go to Zaire (now Democratic Republic of Congo) to do some seminar presentations for their field conference. Betty Greene—one of MAF's first pilots—and Dorothy Mount, executive secretary, were also going. At that time MAF had an agreement with some airlines for tickets at 25% of the regular cost—but one had to travel standby so could never be assured of getting on a certain flight if it was full. I met up with Betty and Dorothy in Paris where we were slated to take the same flight to Kinshasa. The flight was not a daily, so it was important that we were able to get on the flight so as to not be late for the conference. We watched with some anxiety as the regular passengers boarded. Would we make it? Finally, Betty and Dorothy were called to the desk and given boarding passes. Would I make it? Yes! My name was called. I was given the last seat on the airplane.

When I arrived in Paris from the States, we landed at Charles de Gaulle airport. The flight to Zaire left from Orly airport which meant that after overnighting I had to take a taxi to the other side of town. A week later, when I returned from Zaire and overnighted again in Paris, I took a taxi the next morning to the Charles de Gaulle airport.

Going inside, I became frustrated. I could not find my airline counter for check-in. Finally, finding someone who spoke English, I was informed that during the week I was gone, the airline moved to the other airport! Sooo--, frantically, I got another taxi, and we made a bee line back across town to Orly. Fortunately, I had just enough time to make the flight.

An interesting thing happened while in Paris. I had planned to spend a couple of nights both to see the sights, since I would possibly never get back there again, and also rest a little and break up the long trip. I was able to get an air crew rate, so staying at the Intercontinental Hotel cost me about $25 per night.

Having lived in Brazil, I knew Portuguese, but that didn't help a bit in France. The first morning, I went down to the café for breakfast. The maître D' informed me that they were full but there was an older gentleman she was sure would be glad to share his table with me. Arriving at the table, she explained the situation to him. He quickly rose, gestured with his hand and said, *"Bon appetite."* Not knowing what he said, I responded with, "Joe Hopkins." Obviously, there was no conversation.

Next morning, same thing. "Yes, we are full, but I'm sure the older gentleman will be happy to again share his table." Approaching the table, he saw me, jumped up, gestured a welcome, and said, *"Bon appetite."* I responded, "Joe Hopkins." You have probably guessed by now that the same thing happened again the third morning. Yes, but this time, I explained my predicament of not understanding French to the maître D. She laughed and said, "Oh, he is saying 'good appetite'—'enjoy your meal.'" Thinking I'd beat him to the punch this time, I approached his table and blurted out "*Bon appetite*." He jumped up, and responded, "Joe Hopkins."

Although I did go to Zaire by way of Paris, and I did stay at the Intercontinental Hotel, the last part of this paragraph is not a true story. I made it up!

When I first arrived on staff at Moody Aviation, they had, and continued to have, quite a few relatively minor accidents such as ground-loops with the taildraggers and such. Some were flip-overs, however that did a lot of damage.

Moody Aviation training accident

Because of the accident investigation and prevention training I received before leaving MAF, I took on the role of Safety Coordinator in addition to my other

Moody Aviation training accidents

flight instructor responsibilities. I began investigating and documenting each incident and accident—both maintenance and flight. I put together quarterly reports and distributed them to staff and students. We also formed a safety committee with monthly meetings. This had a positive effect. Mishaps were reduced.

In addition, I set up a program of monthly walk-through safety inspections of the facility. I would choose a different staff person each month to walk

Bonus Bucks used in safety incentive

through the facility and make a written list of anything they saw that might be a safety hazard or even an appearance item that needed attention. This information was passed along to the appropriate supervisor of the area affected for correction. Having a different person each month meant that a separate set of eyes with different sensitivities would be looking and perhaps picking up something that another person might miss.

At this time, Moody also had an agreement with the City of Elizabethton to manage the Fixed Base Operation (FBO) for local and transient pilots. Moody students were hired to work there on a part time basis. There was a lot of unnecessary hangar rash—wingtips and tails being bumped into other aircraft or hangar walls. An incentive program I came up with that seemed to work quite well was called "Bonus Bucks." If the employee could go a certain number of hours without damaging an airplane, he would be awarded Bonus Bucks certificates which we printed for the purpose. These could then be redeemed at the FBO or through Moody for books and supplies. The program accomplished its purpose of reducing aircraft damage.

Helmets were now being used by missionary pilots a lot, so I got their use started in the latter part of the Moody student's training. Students, then, would already have their helmet when they went out to serve. We ordered fitting kits for the students, and I probably molded over a 100 pilots' heads while there. The dome-shaped mold would be soaked in hot water to soften it and make it pliable. It was then pressed down over the pilot's

Joe preparing mold for custom fit helmet for Clay Norman

head and allowed to cool and harden before being removed and packed for shipment to the helmet company. We also took measurements of the head to send along with the mold as extra confirmation. By then most of the helmets were being ordered with visors and with headphones and microphone installed.

Our family still had strong ties with the California church family, so one summer they invited us to join them for a camping trip to Tuolumne Meadows in the Sierra Mountains. I could rent a Cessna 210 from Moody at a decent staff rate, so our whole family flew out to California for the adventure. We landed at the Lee Vining airport and were met by some of the group who drove us up the mountain to the campground. They had brought a tent and everything else we needed to make us comfortable since there would not be room in the airplane for it. What a caring group! We settled in and had a really great time fellowshipping, hiking and getting caught up to date with our friends for several days. Back down the mountain, into the Cessna, and away we went winging our way back to Tennessee. Making memories. That's what it's called.

Due to my involvement in aviation safety, not only was I a member of the International Society of Air Safety Investigators (ISASI) but also worked out a school membership for Moody in the Flight Safety Foundation (FSF.) I attended several of their seminar conferences and got to know some of their key people. One year the FSF seminar was to be held in Caracas, Venezuela. I decided to submit a proposal for a presentation entitled "Making Jungle Flying Safer," and it was accepted. Now to get there. After discussing it with Dirk Van Dam, Moody Aviation Director, he decided that we would take Moody's twin-engine Beechcraft Baron and fly to Caracas. That way Elaine could also go. He also invited Merrill Piper, who was the Director of Safety at JAARS.

We left Elizabethton and stopped at Waxhaw, NC to pick up Merrill. Then we flew to West Palm Beach, FL. From there we flew to Port of Prince, Haiti and fueled up for the longest leg of the overwater journey. Weather was good, and we landed in Caracas that afternoon. Being in a small airplane on a big airliner airport presented its challenges in finding a place to park and find our way to customs. In addition to our luggage, I had a big box of handouts for the seminar. Customs seemed hesitant about what to do with the cardboard box and just left us standing there while they went to consult with who-knows-who and who-knows-where.

When they didn't immediately return, we gathered the box and our luggage together and proceeded through, emerging onto the street no worse for the wear. My presentation consisted of a slide presentation with me narrating. There were no boos, so I guess they liked it. The flight back home was a retrace of the flight down except that we were treated to seeing a water spout just off shore and about a half mile to our left during our approach to land at the West Palm Beach airport. After swooping into the JAARS airstrip well after dusk to deliver Merrill, we arrived back in Elizabethton before midnight.

The next FSF seminar I attended was in Rio de Janeiro, Brazil. I also made a presentation at that one. This time travel was via airlines, and I combined it with a trip to Fortaleza, Brazil to visit the Association of Baptists for World Evangelism (ABWE) pilot operating there and to Santa Cruz, Bolivia for a seminar/visit with the South America Mission (SAMAIR) pilots.

As Safety Coordinator for Moody, I thought it would be good to have a safety seminar for the students and staff but also invite anyone else from missions and local pilots to attend. I invited my friend David Hall to do the first one. David was the man who came around to MAF offering to help after they suffered two fatal accidents. He also is the one who got me into the Aircraft Accident Investigation and Prevention course at USC.

This was a success, and we decided to have seminars every two years after that. We always invited a speaker or two from the aviation missions such as JAARS and MAF—names like Glen Mast, Daryl Bussert, Bill Born, Ron Maines—but also landed some perhaps more

Elaine and Joe Hopkins with astronaut Charlie Duke and wife Dottie

famous ones in the process. Some of note were Rick Fowler of the Minerth-Myer Clinic; Capt. John Testrake, the TWA pilot who was hijacked in the Middle-East; Capt. Terry Moose of American Airlines; Dwight McSmith who was with NASA and in charge of their aircraft crash testing program; Capt. Dan Manningham, United Airlines; Capt. Homer Mouden, Flight Safety Foundation; and Charlie Duke, astronaut and moon walker. I could go on.

While I was still with MAF, other missions would sometimes send us their pilots either for an evaluation or for pre-field flight training, and I was involved in a significant portion of those. After I transitioned to Moody, they would sometimes send their pilots to me in Tennessee—often due to the convenience of closeness and their not having to travel across the country to MAF in California. We also developed a Moody Furlough

Refresher Course consisting of ten hours of training for those returning from the field. As I flew with these budding pilots doing the evaluations and pre-field training, and also flying with those returning from the field for furlough and observing often how rusty they were in some areas of their flying, I began to feel there was a need for some kind of continuing education program. One that didn't require them to leave their job on the field but rather we could visit and provide these services on site with minimum disruption of their work. At that time, the missions did not have much— anything—of ongoing proficiency training on the field. In many cases, the pilot would not have anyone looking over his shoulder for four years. Bad habits and rustiness can develop without a person being aware of it. The vision was cloudy, but thoughts were beginning to form in the recesses of my mind.

I wrote letters to about thirty missionary aviation leaders laying out my thoughts on the need and a way to address it. How about an organization that would do safety audits and seminars on-site? Would this fill a need? One respondent expressed some reservation, but the others were all supportive of—and enthusiastic about—the idea. I talked to my boss Dirk Van Dam, and he was supportive. This would mean I would have to resign my faculty position at Moody, since I would not be able to continue my instructor duties and travel around the world, too. What about finances? God always provides when doing His work, right? I resigned, and Dirk hired me as a part-time, time-slip employee to continue to provide safety services to Moody Aviation.

There is a song that says, in reference to the death and resurrection of Lazarus, that even though God may seem to be late by our expectations (four days in this case), He is always on time. For a while, I felt that He was four days late in providing my financial needs. I had envisioned that support for my new program, Mission Safety International, Inc. (MSI), would be forthcoming. It wasn't, and I was disappointed but kept plugging away. The school system had eliminated my wife's job as school nurse due to that position being eliminated, so she started looking for work. I even put out feelers for a local job I could do on an interim basis. Meanwhile, I continued development of the new program. New Tribes Mission Aviation became our first subscribing member. We charged a small annual membership fee. A few supporters started sending a small donations each month. By then, the MSI board had set an approved salary figure for me—if money was available. My procedure for the first several years was to total what money had come in for the month, make sure all current bills were paid, hold aside anything needed for an upcoming trip and other expenses, and whatever was left would be my pay. It took years before I was able to draw anything close to the full approved amount.

My daughter Christy was renting an apartment in town from a man I knew. One day she said, "Daddy, Mr. Akers wants to sell the apartments. You should buy them." What? After the initial shock, I thought, *Well, I don't have any retirement program through MSI and Social Security surely won't be enough. Perhaps, if something could be worked out, this could help with my retirement. Rental income probably won't be enough for me to draw from but it will pay off the mortgage about the time I retire. Then there would be income available, and I would own the building.*

There was a total of four apartments—two large three-bedroom 1500 sq. ft. ones, and two 650 sq. ft. garage apartment types. I talked to the owner, and he made me a good offer of minimal down payment. He offered to finance them himself for the first five years at a monthly payment I could afford with a balloon payment at the end. Dad helped me with the down payment, and I became a landlord. Twenty years later the apartment mortgage was paid off, and shortly thereafter I sold them and put the money into an investment account. One thing that made them more viable was that I was able to manage them and do almost all the maintenance myself. Four days late, but always on time! We serve a great God! Lesson learned: He

Apartments owned by the Hopkins

doesn't just dump it in our lap, but usually expects us to be creative and work for it.

Soon after I bought the apartments, a friend of mine was moving out of town and owned a couple of houses he needed to sell. He was renting them primarily to students enrolled in the Moody Aviation training program. I bought one of them and continued with the tradition. The deal I had with the Moody students was that in exchange for low rent, which basically just covered my mortgage payment, insurance and taxes, they would take care of as much of the maintenance as they could and also, when they moved on, they should have done something to the house to make it better. This worked quite well overall until Moody Aviation closed their program in Elizabethton. I then rented it for a while to my daughter before selling it to her so she could accumulate some equity for the future.

Tenants for the apartments varied substantially over the years from friends and acquaintances to strangers. Over the twenty years of ownership, I was fortunate to have never had over a few months cumulative of vacancy. They essentially stayed full all the time. I never advertised other than putting a For Rent sign in the yard when one became vacant. My overall experience with tenants was positive, with just a few bad apples. The bad apples did such things as move out unannounced leaving a dog locked up inside for nearly a week without food or water, get behind on rent and have to leave, and a couple of times trash the place including doors off the hinges, etc. I only had to legally evict one through the court process. The good ones paid on time and took reasonable care of the property.

I went for many years without a bug problem, but then new tenants brought cockroaches in with their stuff and it took a couple of years of professional treatment to get that under control. I never had a bedbug issue—but almost. Right after I sold the property, one of the back apartment tenants told the new owner that he had bedbugs, but admitted to the new owner that he had never told me. Phew, I was off the hook on that one. I felt bad for the new owner, however, so I wrote a check for several hundred dollars to help with the treatment expense.

I did improvements. The back apartments had electric wall heaters, which can be dangerous if something is left in front of them since their coils got red hot. I replaced them with baseboard heaters. I had vinyl siding installed on the non-brick parts and new double-pane windows installed in all four units—an incredible 68 windows in all! I had central heat and air installed in the two big front units. Some of the hardwood floors were refinished and, of course, painting and the occasional carpet replacement went with the territory.

I had an interesting, and very long, birthday experience. It was during one of my MSI trips to Papua New Guinea for a safety seminar, I had finished and was ready for the return trip home. On this occasion I had made arrangements for Elaine to meet me in Hawaii for a few days. Due to my travels I had enough frequent flyer miles to cover her airfare. My flight back would be stopping in Hawaii. I left Wewak, PNG on the morning of my birthday, October 2, and flew on the airline westbound over to Sentani, Irian Jaya, where I took another short flight north to the island of Biak. Garuda Airlines would be stopping there in the evening on the way to Hawaii. So I had half a day to relax in Biak awaiting the flight. Fortunately, a missionary there had accommodations he made available for missionaries traveling through. Evening came, and I boarded the flight for Hawaii. Still my birthday. After flying all night, I arrived in Honolulu in time to have lunch with Elaine on my birthday! I had crossed the International Date Line so I gained a day. Elaine had just arrived from the mainland. Perfect timing. We had a great time. God is good all the time.

Elaine, ready for our 40th anniversary cruise on the "big red boat"

In the year 2000, we enjoyed another special celebration. Our 40th anniversary. We took a cruise on "The Big Red Boat" as it was nicknamed. The cruise departed from Cape Canaveral to the Bahamas and return. This was a Christian cruise. The gambling tables and bars were shut down. There was a special speaker and lots of southern gospel music groups. This is where we became immersed in gospel music on a serious basis and have enjoyed attending concerts since that time. I like the harmony of gospel music groups, but even more than that, the songs consist of biblical truth and stories.

The year 2010 called for a special celebration for our 50th wedding anniversary. The kids went all out in planning and carrying out the event. Near Elizabethton was an old house called the Butler Mansion. It had been restored and made available for such events. Friends and

family from far and wide showed up, and we had a great celebration.

Elaine and Joe Hopkins celebrating their 50th anniversary in 2010

Joe & Elaine Hopkins with children Judy, Christy, and Steve

The Health Business—

Shaklee Comes into Our Lives

Along about 1977 or so, I had been talking to a friend we had known through MAF during our time in California, and somehow the subject of Shaklee came up. He had been in the business, but suggested we try to find someone local in Tennessee to learn more and possibly get involved. At about the same time my wife, Elaine, found out about the Shaklee business and the health benefits of their vitamin products through Kay Arthur. Kay is the well-known Bible teacher in Chattanooga. She put us in touch with Shaklee sales leaders there, and first thing we knew, we were up and running as sales leaders ourselves in just a few months' time.

Elaine, being the outgoing person she was, and with her contacts through the school system as school nurse, the in-home business grew rapidly. As our group began using the products, they found they were feeling better and they spread the word by telling their friends and "sponsoring them in." We saw health improvements in so many people in our group it would take a separate book to describe them all. My mom had been in very poor health and was at the point that we could hardly read the letters she wrote to us, among other things. She began to feel much better, and her handwriting returned to normal. One lady in Johnson City, TN was literally in a wheelchair before she started on the vitamins. She improved to the point of not only no wheel chair but going on to build her own Shaklee business and qualifying for her own Bonus Car!

In less than a year we qualified for our first Shaklee Bonus Car, an Oldsmobile Cutlass. Over the years we would qualify for five bonus cars—a new one every two or three years. We had four Oldsmobile Delta 88's. Two had a diesel engine. Our last one was a Plymouth Voyager mini-van, which came in handy when we traveled as a family to Disney World in Florida.

We qualified for Shaklee convention trips to San Francisco CA, Scottsdale AZ, Washington DC, New Orleans LA, Greenleaf FL, Chicago IL, Orlando FL, Anaheim CA, and Nashville TN, and even to the Bahamas. For the Bahamas trip, I flew us there in the Moody Beechcraft Baron. It was nice that it had two engines for the overwater crossing. It worked out for Christy to go with us on that trip. Other Shaklee related trips were enjoyed to such places as Pigeon Forge, TN and Fort Lauderdale, FL. We made many memories and new friends.

Eventually, our business began to fade primarily due to one of the sales leaders under us not treating his customers fairly and honestly. He refused to listen to my counsel or that of the Shaklee Company, so he lost his business and in the process blamed us for his problems. By then we were getting older, I was occupied with MSI business and lots of travel, so we didn't put the effort back into it to build it back up. Today, although we don't have an official business, I continue to use the products and have several customers that still appreciate me providing their products for them.

Local Ministries

As the Christian and Missionary Alliance church of Elizabethton that got its start in our living room began to grow, both Elaine and I continued to have involvement. She was the key person for many years in getting the church nursery established. Her love for the babies and little kids showed through in both the physical aspects of the facility and the welcoming environment. She would also play key roles with involvement in the Alliance Women and serving as head deaconess. I served on the Governing Board and Elder Board for many years and a couple of years as acting treasurer. Due to my MSI travel, I was not always able to dedicate as much time and effort into those roles as I would have liked.

In the early 1980s a neighbor convinced me I should join the local Gideon Camp group. As an instructor/teacher at Moody, I would qualify. I still am a member and have enjoyed the blessings of attending Gideon conventions, participating in Scripture distributions at hotels, universities and local schools and the fellowship our local camp provided through monthly meetings and the weekly prayer breakfasts on Sunday mornings. I am not a morning person, but never had a problem getting up earlier than usual on Sunday mornings for those meetings, which started at 7:30 A.M.

I had the opportunity to join men's prayer breakfasts and other such organizations but declined, realizing that practically all my associations and activities involved other Christians. About that time, I found out about the local ham radio club. Since I had been wanting to do more with my ham radio experience, I decided to join. The added benefit would be that perhaps a non-Christian or two might be positively influenced by my life. There were plenty of non-Christians in the group all right, but I soon found out there were also some fellow believers as well.

Elaine Lamberson Hopkins

1937 – 2020

Sixty years, eight months and two days. That's how long it was from when we were joined as husband and wife until the Lord took her home. We became as one and had the privilege of serving together all those wonderful years.

Elaine was born in New York. Her very young mother gave her up right away to foster care. When she was five years old, she was adopted. Her adoptive mother was a strong Christian but the father, not so much. After graduation from high school, her dad insisted that she train for a profession. It was decided she would enroll at the University of Rochester and take nurse training. She graduated with certification as a Registered Nurse.

Her mom had all along wanted her to get Bible training, so Elaine then enrolled at the Moody Bible Institute in Chicago. Her thinking was she could then serve as a missionary nurse. This plan got modified after meeting me at Moody. I say modified, instead of cancelled, because we did go to the mission field and she was able to put her nursing skills to good use.

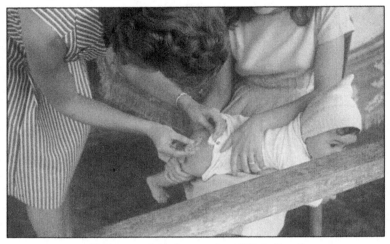

Elaine exercising her nursing skills in Brazil

Elaine had to endure a number of health challenges over the years. During our time in Brazil, she had a miscarriage and ultimately a hysterectomy. When we moved to the northeast coast of Brazil, she became sick with what was first thought to be malaria but later was diagnosed as a severe urinary tract and kidney infection. This led to us returning to the USA for care and treatment.

After moving to Tennessee, she had abdominal surgery and also knee surgery for a torn meniscus. Later, she required a knee replacement and cataract surgery. All this took a toll on her body, but she pushed herself and kept going as long as she was able. In retrospect, there were warning signs that all was not well.

About three years after we sold our house and moved to an independent living retirement center, she was attending a piano concert that was being presented for the residents when she suddenly slumped to the side. I was away at another meeting. The other residents thought at first she had fallen asleep, but when they were unable to get her to respond, they called the rescue squad. They took her to the hospital where she stayed overnight and underwent many tests. Not finding any real cause for the fainting, she was released. Looking back, I feel she had a mini-stroke. This is based on the fact that a year or so later after her fall and hip replacement, and not being able to recover well, she had an MRI which showed she had experienced numerous mini-strokes over time that left her with significant brain damage.

The fall and broken hip, which turned out to be the beginning of the end, started when she was going to a memorial service at the veterans' cemetery. She rode with friends, and as she was stepping out of the back seat of the car, she fell. It's unclear whether she tripped or perhaps had a mini-stroke. In any case, she was in terrible pain and was unable to get up, so 911 was called. The ambulance took her to the nearby hospital. X-rays showed a broken hip, so surgery was scheduled for the next day. I was in Brazil on MSI business when this happened, but fortunately was on my way home and arrived about an hour before she went in for surgery.

Several days after surgery, arrangements were made for her to go to a rehab center where she spent the next twenty-three days. She progressed to being able to walk with a walker and was released to return to our apartment, where continued rehab treatment would take place. After a couple of months, she still showed no progress, and in fact showed signs of getting worse. Then, overnight, she lost the use of her legs completely and became bedridden. This paralysis eventually worked its way up to where she gradually lost the use of both arms and hands. Hospice had been called in by now and was a big help but, then, due to the Covid pandemic, our facility would no longer even allow hospice in to help. I was on my own—complete caregiver for weeks. Just before she passed away, Hospice attendants were allowed to come back in on a limited basis.

She didn't suffer with a lot of pain until close to the end. Where an occasional Tylenol was all she needed in the beginning, I had to resort to the morphine for the last week or so. I awakened about 5:00 a.m. on Friday, September 25 to find that she was no longer breathing but had been received into the loving arms of Jesus. New body. No more suffering.

The following account is taken from my Christmas letter.

I was in the terminal of the Rio airport having just arrived on a flight from Brasilia. It was Friday, October 11, 2019. The MSI safety audit of one of our member organizations was complete. After a long walk and checking departure schedule screens along the way I found my departure gate area. However, my flight to Atlanta would not be for several hours. Finding a seat I settled back to enjoy the view overlooking aircraft and hangars.

On the horizon beyond those, I could see Sugarloaf Mountain to the left, and the huge Christ the Redeemer statue to the right perched on Corcovado Mountain. Memories flooded my mind as I thought back to the time I was there fifty-four years earlier. How different everything looked then. I had flown a Cessna to Rio from the center of Brazil bringing a missionary nurse who had been diagnosed with a brain tumor to catch a flight back to her homeland in Europe for treatment.

While reminiscing and enjoying the view my phone rang. It was son Steve advising that my wife Elaine had fallen and was at the emergency room for x-rays. Soon he called back with the news that she had a broken hip and was scheduled for surgery the following morning.

Thanks to a kind, understanding Delta agent in Atlanta putting me on an earlier flight to Tennessee I arrived at the hospital about an hour before surgery. Thus began a long period—two weeks short of a year—filled with rehab, progress and regression, full time caregiving, covid lockdowns, hospice and finally release as she went to be with Jesus on September 25.

During that time, many prayers went up, visits were made, cards and flowers brought or sent, and love was shown. Thank you all. God bless each one of you.

Thanksgiving was different. Christmas will be different. The memories of my sweetheart will remain strong and comforting. To borrow a phrase from my dear friend Dr. Charles Shepson in his book *From My Grieving Heart to Yours,* upon the passing of his wife, "Her star will always be uniquely fixed in my sky." But we continue to trust Jesus—the author and finisher of our faith. Let's all be ready for the end whether it is our turn going on to glory or being caught up to be with Him at His imminent return. Christmas provides our hope—the birth of our Savior.

   Merry Christmas to you.
   Joe Hopkins

My Personal Testimony

in a (Big) Nutshell

I was blessed to have Christian parents and grow up in a Christian home and church environment. Because of this, I heard the good news early of how we all are sinners and that Jesus Christ came to earth, was crucified and raised from the dead for my own sins. I accepted Him as my personal Savior at the age of nine. Thankfully, I was spared the problems and sinful ways so often encountered by those who don't hear about or come to know Jesus personally until later in life.

We had many missionaries speak in our church and visit in our home, so I knew there was a need for believers to go tell the good news to those who needed to hear about Jesus. Not all missionaries are preachers. Some serve in other ways such as the medical field. Since I had interests and skills in the technical area, I took training in the aviation field and served many years in missions as a pilot and mechanic. My family did this in Brazil, Honduras and later in the USA, where I trained future missionary pilots first at the MAF base in California and then in Tennessee at Moody Aviation.

I have a friend, Charlie Duke, who walked on the moon. Course corrections were necessary for getting him there and safely back home again. Slight miscalculations, and their capsule could have bounced off the earth's atmosphere and been lost in space forever. When I flew my family from California to Tennessee in 1972, I made course corrections along the way in order to arrive exactly at the Elizabethton airport. Life's that way. God brings mid-course corrections as he steers us toward the goals he has for us.

I was born at a very early age but will start my story here at seventeen as a senior in high school. I had dabbled in electronics and had my amateur radio license. I also had taken a couple of flying lessons. In order to combine the two interests, I thought perhaps I should be a radio operator in the Air Force, since I wore glasses and didn't think I could qualify as a pilot.

Dad saw an ad in Moody Monthly magazine about Moody's flight program and suggested I consider going to Moody and learning to fly. He had already said that regardless of what a person does, he or she should have Bible school training. To make what could be a long story shorter, I went to Moody in Chicago and first took the missionary radio course and then missionary aviation. Oh yes, I also took a wife!

After working for a year or so to build aviation experience and pay off bills, we boarded the ship along with our first two children, Judy and Steve, for what we assumed would be a lifetime on the mission field.

After two years in Brazil and Elaine's significant struggles with health problems, we sold most of what we had and returned to the States to seek medical treatment.

This was mid-course correction number one. MAF put me to work in their training department and eventually I became Manager of Technical Training.

We spent the next five and a half years on MAF's home staff in Fullerton, CA. This included a half-year in Honduras, where we filled in for a pilot home on furlough. It also included an opportunity to get accident investigation and prevention training at the University of Southern California. This developed into a strong interest in safety for me.

During one of the Moody cross-country training flight visits to MAF, the Moody Aviation Director mentioned that they needed someone on their flight staff with field experience. The Lord spoke to me strongly about that, and soon the Hopkins family, which now also included Christy and a cat, were in the Cessna 210 winging our way toward Tennessee. That was in 1972 and marked mid-course correction number two.

It might be helpful to point out here that it was the strong sense of the Lord's leading me to Moody that kept me there when the ride was not so smooth. In fact, when weighing the pros and cons of whether to leave MAF, the cons won out on paper, but ultimately the decision to move was based on the strong sense of God's leading in the matter.

While on the Moody flight staff training missionary pilots and evaluating pilots for other missions, I sensed a need for some kind of continuing education program for the mechanics and pilots on the field. After seeking counsel from several key people in missionary aviation I felt the need strongly enough to give up the security of Moody's salary and benefits after ten years there. I took another step of faith. Mid-course correction number three.

In 1983 I founded Mission Safety International, Inc. (MSI) in order to help reduce accidents in missionary aviation. The Lord has blessed these efforts, and we believe that many lives have been saved as a result.

I "just knew" that the Lord would provide my full support in honor of my dedication, but it didn't turn out quite that way. It was a financial struggle for many years. Through Elaine working, our Shaklee business, and sometimes even mowing lawns for extra income, we managed, although frankly there were times when I was afraid we wouldn't have money to pay our bills.

I often told the Lord and others that when the day came that I couldn't pay my bills that I was "out of here." That day hasn't come yet. Even though I had no retirement plan through MSI, "His favor is for a Lifetime." Matthew 6:33 says that if we seek first the kingdom of God and His righteousness, all these things shall be added unto us. I took that as my life verse at an early age and have found God to be faithful to His promises. There may be other mid-course corrections to come, but hey, bring them on! I have every assurance that He will get me home—safely.

I have lived over three-fourths of my expected life span and am here to tell you that living the life of a believer is the only way to go. God will bless you in ways hard to imagine and provide for your needs as you "seek first the kingdom of God and His righteousness."

I am so glad that becoming a believer is not complicated. The Bible tells us that if we believe in the Lord Jesus Christ and accept Him into our lives as personal

Savior, we will have eternal life, that is, go to be with God when we die. It does not get any better than that!

PART TWO

The MSI Story

Introduction

The task for the day was to continue preparing the new guy for his first term of service as a missionary pilot.

Departing Fullerton CA airport through the murky sky—as in Los Angeles smog in the summer time, our Cessna 206 broke out on top of the smog at about the usual two thousand feet and headed east under blue sky with 50+ miles visibility.

The more detailed task was to practice takeoffs and landings at a very narrow and short airstrip. Arriving overhead we carefully observed the unpaved runway below and I allowed the trainee to follow the previously taught procedure of checking a marginal airstrip before landing. This included circles and passes at progressively lower altitudes looking for obstructions, holes or other impediments on the airstrip, slope of the strip, wind direction and velocity.

Several landings and takeoffs were performed. During one takeoff, just before liftoff, I cut the engine power to idle to gauge my trainee's reaction and performance in aborting the takeoff. Well done! As we continued to taxi toward the end of the airstrip for a takeoff in the opposite direction suddenly I spied a small child, probably five or six years old, walking directly toward the plane and its spinning propeller. As I yelled "stop the engine!" we both frantically grabbed levers and switches and stood on the brakes. The prop stopped its rotation just inches from the kid.

I quickly jumped out, gathered the child into my arms and deposited him with the adult onlookers at the edge of the airstrip with a stern warning to all that they must remain clear of the airstrip at all times.

Deciding it would be prudent at this point to take a break and settle the adrenalin flow, we pulled out our lunch bags and thermos while seated on the ground in the shade of the wing.

Refreshed and ready to continue, I offered a ride to three of the adult bystanders since we needed to practice with near maximum weight in the airplane. They eagerly accepted and soon were securely strapped in their seats. What came next was like anyone's worst nightmare.

We positioned the plane at the very beginning of the airstrip, at which time I reminded the trainee to hold the brakes until the engine reached nearly full power. We would need the full length of the airstrip to get off with the extra weight. Rolling down the strip, I sensed that we were not accelerating as we should. Glancing down, I noticed the trainee had taken his hand off the throttle and that it had backed out slightly, thus reducing power. As I pointed this out, he quickly pushed the throttle fully in and continued the takeoff. I'm now thinking, *Should we abort? Will he decide to abort?* All the while the end of the airstrip was approaching and airspeed was still not adequate for liftoff.

The takeoff attempt continued and we just staggered off as the end of the airstrip slid beneath us. We were almost too slow to climb. Gradually we gained a few feet of altitude with the stall warning horn blaring continuously indicating the wing was just barely flying. We needed more airspeed.

"Lower the nose a bit to get more airspeed," I advised.

"I can't. The control wheel won't go forward," came the slightly panicked reply. I helped push the control wheel from my dual controls but it wouldn't budge. The airplane began to shake, indicating it was about to quit flying. It tilted nose down and rolled slightly left. We were going to crash!

At that very instant my full bladder awakened me and told me I needed to go to the bathroom. Drenched in sweat, I rolled out of bed and looked at the clock. 5:05 a.m.

It was my worst nightmare and fortunately not a reality. However, it reminded me of those missionary pilots, many of whom I had known personally, whose worst nightmare became a reality. The ones who deliberately or inadvertently got into cloud and struck "cumulo-granite," or who took off overloaded for the conditions and ended up in a fireball off the end of the airstrip, or attempted to abort a landing at a no-go-around airstrip coming to rest in a heap of crumpled aluminum. Every situation in the above narrative I have either experienced or written about in an accident report.

In the next pages, I will give some history of missionary aviation from my perspective, explain how Mission Safety International, Inc. (MSI) came into being and how missionary aviation has changed over the years, talk about progress made in making it safer, and then share some of my experiences from the years of doing safety seminars and safety audits around the world.

The Missionary Aviation Evolution

Having outlived my allotted "three-score and ten," I have participated in and observed quite a lot in the field of missionary aviation. Most of it good, even very good, but also some aspects that would scare the fleas off of a mangy dog. These reflections have their beginnings in the early to mid-1960s and continue to the present.

But first, starting right after World War II, when missionary aviation began to really take off, so to speak, there were some major potholes in the runway. Some felt that the way to go was for a missionary to come back from the field, get his private license and an airplane to take back to the field. Unfortunately, due to his lack of experience this sometimes resulted in tragedy due to an accident.

Fortunately, some, like Paul Robinson who founded Moody Aviation, realized that what was really needed was a highly trained pilot/mechanic who could dedicate his efforts to operating the aircraft professionally full time while serving multiple missionaries in a given area. This had the advantage of allowing the missionary to dedicate his time and effort to what he was trained to do, that of being a missionary. Having said that, I know some who have successfully combined aviation with their other missionary activities.

Those early days had hits and misses. Hits like the pilots coming from a farming background. This often fostered dedication to the task, creativity, ingenuity, and problem solving. Hits like those who recognized lines of authority, following the rules, good ethics, and were relationship builders. Misses sometimes reared their ugly heads by those whom we might charitably call "cowboys." Their mindset was that they were out there to "serve the Lord" and whatever it took to get the job done (as they perceived it) was fair game. This is the mindset that causes one to fly with overloaded aircraft, below prescribed weather minimums, or with inadequately maintained aircraft.

Since all of missionary aviation was new, there was a learning curve. The mission organization was usually relatively small and thus via personal interactions and correspondence, the pilot or mechanic had the minds of their leaders fairly well and they operated in harmony. These personnel were new and inexperienced but so was the program which allowed them to grow together. Today, the programs are highly developed operating at a high level and thus require new personnel to gradually work themselves up to that level through orientation training and good, gradual field checkouts. This brought about the need for Operations Manuals, Standards and Controls. I wonder, too, if the young applicants of today require more structure due to the fact their whole life experience has been in a structured school environment as opposed to the maturing process such as growing up on a farm or coming out of the military.

Piper Super Cub landing on small mission airstrip

Early airstrips were carved out of jungles and mountainsides to accommodate the small aircraft of that time such as Piper Super Cubs, Family Cruisers, Cessna 180s, etc. seating two to four people. Today most missionary aircraft are much larger and some can seat eight to twenty people. Failure to upgrade airstrips accordingly would sometimes lead to accidents. Piloting skills today for flying a turbine Caravan, Kodiak, King Air, or helicopter are much more demanding. The same goes for maintenance skills of the mechanic. Early pilots seldom had an instrument flying rating or flight instructor certificate. Today the majority have both.

Perhaps I am sounding like I am being very harsh on the people out on the front lines. I don't want to. Sometimes it was the system, or lack thereof. Aviators would go overseas for a four year assignment and operate without oversight from others. This allowed them to lose

Replica of Nate Saint's Ecuador airplane of the 1950's next to modern Kodiak used in today's mission operations (Picture taken at Oshkosh WI)

certain skills due to lack of use or discipline. Later, missions established programs for periodic recurrency, proficiency checks and training during their term on the field. Of course, MSI came on the scene and has contributed greatly in safe operations primarily through providing safety information, seminars and safety audits.

Believe it or not, there was competition between organizations. Some took a dim view of others or felt themselves to be superior. This resulted in lack of cooperation. As an example, I am aware of one mission that moved to a location where another aviation organization already had an established program and set up their own hangar and flight operation next door on the same airport! All because they wanted to serve their own missionaries with their own aircraft. This problem has largely been eliminated over the years and a lot of the credit belongs to an organization called the International Association of Mission Aviation (IAMA). The effort wasn't an organization at first, but began simply by several key missionary aviation leaders recognizing the need for cooperation and getting together periodically for fellowship and discussions. One of the first meetings that I remember being aware of was held at the Missionary Aviation Fellowship (MAF) headquarters in Fullerton CA in the late 1960s. A couple of the organizations being represented that I remember in addition to MAF, were the School of Missionary Aviation (SOMA), San Diego CA, and the Jungle Aviation and Radio Service (JAARS), Waxhaw NC. Today, IAMA has grown to be an official organization with many members and worldwide influence. Typically, IAMA sponsors an annual conference which is hosted by one of their member organizations on a rotating basis at their headquarters location. The result has been significant cooperation, respect, and sharing of resources between organizations.

The transition has been (mostly) fun to watch as the mission aviation community has transitioned toward cooperation with each other, and from reactive safety to proactive safety. Busted airplanes and broken bodies are something we would like to do without in our efforts to make Christ known to the world.

Milestones and Accomplishments

Usually we start out by celebrating a tenth anniversary as a significant milestone in events such as marriage or founding of an organization. Then typically we celebrate the 25, 50 and centennials. Markers are useful for reminding us of progress made or special blessings from the Lord.

The Old Testament particularly points this out in the stories of Moses and Joshua and how they erected pillars of stones as a reminder to all who saw them of how God parted the waters of the Jordan River and other miracles He performed for them.

As I look back over thirty-seven years of MSI history, I see many events and even milestones showing God's blessing on our ministry.

While working as a flight instructor with the Moody Bible Institute missionary aviation training program, the Lord laid on my heart the idea that there was a need for a continuing education program of training and proficiency for missionary mechanics and pilots. At that time many would be operating overseas for up to four years without opportunity for much, if any, recurrency training or check-ups. I wrote to about 30 organizations outlining my concerns and proposal. The responses were almost 100 percent supportive and enthusiastic. Thus began the journey of stepping out in faith to make something happen as I resigned from my position at Moody Aviation. Alongside me, three others, Ed Essick, a local businessman and pilot, Captain Terry Moose with American Airlines, and Dwight McSmith of NASA agreed to the need and thus became the founding board members. A few months later, in August of 1983, MSI became an official nonprofit organization with IRS tax exempt status.

The first ministry trip was to the Philippines for Tribal Air Communications, which later became New Tribes Mission Aviation, and now Ethos 360. They became our first subscribing member. After performing a safety seminar for them in Manila and then audits for their three flight programs, I was also able to jump on over to Irian Jaya (now Papua) for a visit with the JAARS and MAF folks. Samaritans Purse was instrumental in getting us started by providing me with counsel on setting up the organization and also funding a portion of that first trip.

Other mission organizations began signing up for MSI's services and soon we were making fairly regular international trips to work with them. Our services then, and now, consist primarily of safety seminars, safety audits (originally called safety surveys), being on call for accident investigations and providing periodic safety information through various publications and mishap reports. The mishap reports turned out to be an effective accident prevention tool as evidenced by one of our subscriber pilots telling me that when making safety related decisions regarding a flight or maintenance action he would think, "Hmmm... I wonder how this would look written up in an MSI report." In the early days before many missions had their own training and proficiency programs I was often asked to fly with the pilots to fulfill the requirements for their mission proficiency checks or for the FAA Biennial Flight Review, etc.

Operating on a low cash budget, MSI depends greatly on volunteers. These volunteers, which I call the lifeblood of the organization, are highly trained and qualified individuals who share our vision of mission aviation safety to the point they are willing to donate their time and resources. In fact, their donated services are typically valued at between $100,000 and $150,000 per

Missionary Aviation Worldwide

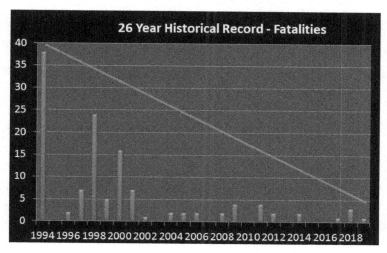

year. They help with the audits and seminars and even their counsel when needed. They are airline pilots, former missionary mechanics and pilots, industrial safety experts, safety consultants, etc. For example, Mr. McSmith, one of our founding board members, was with NASA for about 40 years and was in charge of an extensive aircraft crash testing program. After one of his presentations showing the dynamics of a crash, one would be convinced beyond doubt that crashing an aircraft was definitely to be avoided!

We have had seminar speakers such as another founding board member Captain Terry Moose of American Airlines, and Captain Dan Manningham, author and pilot with United Airlines. We also had John Testrake, the TWA pilot whose plane was hijacked in the Middle East, Charlie Duke, astronaut who walked on the moon, and their wives. Joe Boxmeyer, 3M Corporation flammable liquids and static electricity expert, could spark interest and light up your life with his explosive demonstrations. (Interesting side note: When we traveled together, someone started calling us "Pilot Joe" and "Pyro Joe" to distinguish between the two of us.)

We've had Rick Fowler, of Minirth Meyer Clinic, Tony Kern, lecturer and author of numerous books and articles related to safety, Homer Mouden with the Flight Safety Foundation, and others too numerous to mention. We continue to add to the list as new contacts are made.

To date, I and other MSI staff members have traveled to over 40 countries from Africa and Asia, to South America and the Pacific area. Did you know that when we did a study several years ago it was determined that there were over 500 mission aviation pilots and mechanics, and aviation missions operating approximately

330 aircraft? We also work with missionary aviation training schools (at last count there's another 345 pilots and 160 aircraft) not only to help them operate as safely as possible, but also to help make sure their students are learning safety principles and practices right from the start of their training which will carry over into their careers.

One of my early-days dreams was the hope that something could be worked out with insurance companies to give our members a discount. Didn't turn out quite like I envisioned but something even better eventually came along. It's called AIRMAP for Aviation Insurance and Risk Management Alliance Program. This program has been in play for several years now and, in a nutshell, provides excellent insurance coverage with possible premium rebate rewards in return for good behavior—read, didn't tear up aircraft! Participants must be pre-approved, must be subscribing members of MSI, and must have a safety audit every three years. This keeps MSI hopping in completing the audits since we have to average about one audit each month in order to keep up. Again, let me say it. We couldn't do it without our professional volunteers!

As I think back on how the Lord has provided for MSI over the years, several milestones come to mind. As I said earlier, I gave up my position as flight instructor at Moody. However, Dirk Van Dam, Moody Aviation Director at the time, was very supportive of what I was trying to do so he allowed me to use my old office space and also hired me, part-time, as Moody's Safety Coordinator. This gave me some income as I began to develop support from other sources. Several years later the need for office help arose since I was away on trips often.

Don Axford, who had retired from business in Canada had a son enrolled at Moody Aviation and heard I needed help. He and his wife moved to Elizabethon, TN and volunteered to help us full time for two years until his son graduated. This meant the office space at Moody was no longer adequate. I found there was office space available in downtown Elizabethton but didn't know how we would pay for it. One of our board members came, looked at it, and suggested I offer $1,000 rent paid up front for a year and said, if accepted, he would pay for it. It was, and he did! Don Axford proved to be a very valuable office manager and researcher which helped tremendously in getting us established more on our own.

Another valuable resource has been, and continues to be, Dr. Harold Berk. Harold edits and produces our *Safety Net* publication. He did our first ones in black & white in the beginning years but has now progressed to the beautifully done color editions. It's been 30 years and counting. Harold comes well qualified having served as a missionary pilot and field director with Mission Aviation Fellowship (MAF) in Brazil in the beginning days of that program. Later, he returned to the USA, served as a college dean, got his Doctorate, ran his own diesel pump business, and owned and flew his own Piper Twin Comanche for many years. Harold is only in his early 90's so we look forward to many more years of his excellent work!

Then there are Steve Quigg and wife Gail. Steve was a student of mine at Moody. I later visited them in Nigeria where they were operating a missionary flight program and performed an audit. After that they were assigned to another African country but got "kicked out" (not for malfeasance but due to political turmoil.) While they were back in the USA wondering what was next, I called to see if they might be willing to work with MSI in the interim. Turns out they were. Steve and Gail were put on loan to MSI by their mission and they both traveled extensively with and for us doing the seminars and audits. Sadly, after several years their mission wanted them back. Gladly, after about four years they are again back with MSI as of late 2019.

Other current staff consist of Robert King who is full time and formerly served in Papua New Guinea in maintenance with JAARS, Glen Ferguson and Lyle Reffey who are both on loan from JAARS for part of their time, and Jeanette Hill, office secretary. Fergusons served in Brazil and Reffeys served in Papua New Guinea as pilot/mechanics. So, three full-time, two part-time and two on loan. That's the lean-and-mean MSI team.

I had only limited success with fundraising such as grant applications but the Crowell Foundation gave us $25,000 in memory of Paul Robinson (Moody Aviation founder) who was a strong MSI advocate. We did several mailings to owners of the Cessna type aircraft used on the mission field and the Lord blessed us with several significant responses. Their financial support continues to today. Other support comes from membership fees, personalized staff support and general donations. The previously mentioned AIRMAP program provides funds toward our expenses of doing the safety audits.

An interesting funds provision came from one who wished to remain anonymous and wanted only to be referred to as "Bob." Bob was diagnosed with terminal cancer and was in the process of settling his affairs. He invited me to come by his house one day for a visit and asked me how he could help. I told him I had several options for him to consider. I started out low with a couple of projects which only involved several hundred dollars but then finished by saying that what would help most was helping replenish our dwindling cash on hand to carry out our work. I told him I had calculated the total present need and it came to $29,000. Without hesitation, Bob got up, went to another room, and came back with his checkbook. Handing me the check, I was overwhelmed—it was for $29,000.

Our board members over the years have been great. Each has something special to contribute. As they leave, mostly due to 9 years continuous service requiring that they rotate off, others step up to the plate to serve in their own unique and God-given way. The same could be said for those on our International Advisory Council—those who serve by name recognition, active involvement, or promoting MSI within their sphere of influence.

As the new century of the 2000's came and I realized that becoming old, decrepit and toothless was approaching in my life, the search started for my replacement. Chuck Henson, former field pilot who served in Bolivia and Papua New Guinea with New Tribes Mission Aviation (now called Ethnos 360), graciously served as MSI president for a couple of years. Then, in late 2004, Jon Egeler came in as President/CEO. Jon grew up in Africa as the son of missionaries. He went back there and served as missionary pilot/mechanic with Africa Inland Mission (AIMAIR) before later taking on a staff position at Moody Aviation. MSI has enjoyed significant growth and influence under Jon's leadership. I, meanwhile, becoming more old, a bit decrepit, but still having all my teeth, have been blessed to be able to continue serving with MSI as treasurer, bookkeeper, and with occasional other tasks such as safety audits.

PART THREE

MSI Trips and Experiences

My First Trip

One of the questions on the MSI safety survey (now called audit) is about the life goals of the person being interviewed. The response I received from Phil Koop, aviation technician at the Aritao Philippines base, struck me as profound and has always stuck with me. "I didn't come out here to fix radio problems. I came here to prevent problems from happening," he responded. He continued, "I don't want the pilot to have the stress of dealing with a non-functioning radio if there is anything I can do to prevent it." Wow.

My first overseas ministry trip for MSI took place in 1984 and initially was to be in the Philippines to do a safety seminar and safety audit for Tribal Air/Communications (TAC), which later transitioned into being called New Tribes Aviation and now Ethnos 360 Aviation. Considering I would be in the Pacific Rim, I decided to add a side trip to visit Mission Aviation Fellowship (MAF) and JAARS (formerly known as Jungle Aviation and Radio Service) in West Irian, which later was changed to Irian Jaya and is now called Papua. What's with all these name changes?

We started in Manila with a safety seminar held in a back room of Mrs. Ho's Chinese restaurant. I about drove the TAC program manager crazy with all my requests for

Joe presenting at first MSI seminar - Philippines

equipment for the seminar. I needed an overhead projector, 16mm movie projector, and filmstrip projector to handle all my different media types. He did a yeoman's job in getting them all together for me.

After the seminar, I traveled to their three aviation bases for the safety audits. First stop was in northern Luzon at the Aritao base, then over to the island of Palawan, and finally down to the base in

Helio Courier ready for takeoff from steep airstrip

Mindanao. Each stop had its unique experience.

In Luzon, I flew with the pilot in their Helio Courier out to one of the missionary bases. After seeing the slope and shortness of the airstrip, I was glad we were in the Helio which was known for its super short-field capabilities.

Getting off the airline in Puerto Princesa, Palawan, I had the "pleasure" of riding in the baggage-compartment-modified-into-third-seat of a Super Cub to the TAC base further south. For my return to Puerto Princesa, I soon was *wishing* for the baggage compartment seat of the Super Cub. Instead, I was on a bus for about a six hour ride. The bus was full of people and cargo, including on top of the bus. The seats were designed for one and a half people, so I sat with half my anatomy on the seat and the other half on

Joe rode this bus for about six hours - Philippines

the cargo that filled the aisle. When we got within an hour or so of Puerto Princesa, we came to a bridge that had nearly washed out. Not knowing whether it would support the bus or not, the driver had all the passengers disembark and walk across while he drove the bus over empty. Fortunately, all made it across.

At the base in Mindanao I had the "privilege" of riding in the second seat of a Super Cub surrounded by canvas bags of cargo, which I was to throw out the door at the proper time when we were over the missionary's drop zone. On our safety surveys we always ask to fly with the pilots on operational flights to observe them in the real world. Fortunately, this pilot was up to the job, and I am here to write about it.

Joe preparing for supply air drops to missionaries

After finishing the job in the Philippines, I took the airline down to Irian Jaya, Indonesia. Many of my friends were there working with both JAARS and MAF. I was asked to do a courtesy flight evaluation with a pilot or two while there, and I got to see several parts of the island and the airstrips the missions were using. My visit to the offices of JAARS and MAF in Sentani left me with a sobering memory. One which causes me to think often how God works in mysterious ways we just can't comprehend. In the JAARS office, I noticed a number of plaques on the wall commemorating the various safety aspects of their operations. Next door, in the MAF office I was greeted with numerous plaques in memory of pilots who had lost their lives while serving. I'm certainly not being judgmental here. That was at a specific time in history. Both missions have had their successes and losses. Nevertheless, it spurred my resolve to see future missionary aviation talking about a **safety** record rather than an **accident** record.

I enjoyed getting to Wamena in the highlands in the area of *Cannibal Valley* fame. In fact, one of the pilots I stayed with in Bokandini had a copy of the book, and I

Wamena airport in highlands of Papua

marveled as I sat on the porch re-reading much of the book while overlooking the very area of the story. This is also the area where missionary aviation had much of its beginnings through the work of a pilot with the Christian and Missionary Alliance.

I also had the opportunity to meet some of the locals, thanks to a tour around town with MAFer Dave Ketchum. Unfortunately, I can't say the two guys in this picture became my friends, since they were unhappy that we were not willing to pay their asking price for me to take their photo. At least we didn't get a spear in the back as we walked away!

Two of the locals in Papua

Leaving my thoroughly enjoyable visit to Irian, I retraced my path back to Manila and on home to the USA, thus ending the first ever MSI safety seminar/safety survey trip.

Longest Trip Time-Wise

I always liked to join efforts with others and also have others join in with me. I needed to do a trip to Kenya for a safety seminar. In talking with George Fletcher, who was JAARS safety officer at the time, we worked out a plan. JAARS needed safety surveys (audits) in a couple of African countries, so it was decided to combine our efforts and do the seminars and surveys in Liberia, Cameroon, and Kenya. Speakers, in addition to George and myself, would be Captain Terry Moose of American Airlines (and founding MSI board member), and Glen Mast of JAARS. As a bonus blessing, Terry took his wife Mary and I was able to take my dad along as observer. We would be gone for nearly four weeks.

First stop was Liberia for a seminar for JAARS. All went well with mission accomplished. We also had an interesting visit to the local markets including those selling ivory—which was not an issue then like it is today. It was in Liberia where, in all my years of travel, I had my only incident of baggage pilfered. A VHS tape was stolen from one of my soft-sided bags. On it was a presentation about management principles. The flight was somewhat delayed in departing, so I guess that gave someone in the baggage handling department time to go through stuff.

On our way to our next stop in Cameroon, we had a layover in Ivory Coast where we enjoyed a short visit with Wycliffe personnel at their base.

MSI seminar in Cameroon - note headsets used for French translation

In Cameroon the seminar was a big deal. JAARS had invited local government and aviation people to attend along with the missionary aviation community. We submitted our presentation papers ahead of time for translation into French. JAARS/Wycliffe arranged for a live simultaneous translator speaking through earphones to those who only knew French. After the seminar we completed the safety survey before continuing on to Kenya. The flight was on a relatively unknown African airline. The airplane was an old Boeing 707. Terry Moose flew this type airplane during part of his career with the airlines. I wondered what he was thinking when, just before taxi, one of the pilots came back through the cabin toward the rear, lifted a panel in the floor to check on who-knows-what, and then hurriedly returned to the cockpit. Whatever

172

it was didn't prevent us from safely arriving at our next destination of Nairobi.

The final part of the project was to apply our safety efforts to the missionary aviation folks in and around Kenya. African Inland Mission Aviation (AIM-AIR) was our host. After being in the hot, low-lying areas of western Africa, it was refreshing to have a few days of balmy, drier weather in Nairobi above 7,000 feet. Weather in Nairobi can sometimes be deceiving. I remembered from a previous trip, that even though it is near the equator, I had slept with my socks on due to the cold in spite of it being July! Although Dad was in his late 70s he did well, thoroughly enjoyed the trip, and had lots to talk about when he got home.

Longest Trip by Mileage

Probably the longest trip in terms of miles traveled was the one in 1990 when the team traveled from Tennessee and other home towns to Atlanta, Hawaii, Sydney Australia, Cairns Australia, Port Moresby Papua New Guinea (PNG), Goroka PNG, Mt. Hagen PNG, Port Moresby PNG, Cairns Australia, Alice Springs Australia, Darwin Australia, Gove Australia, Cairns Australia, Sydney Australia, Hawaii, Atlanta, and home. A total of about 30,000 miles!

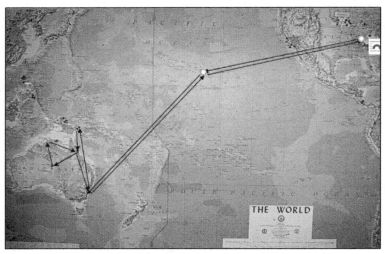

World map showing Joe's longest MSI trip travel - 30,000 miles!

A special member of our team on this trip was Joe Boxmeyer. Joe worked for the 3M Corporation as an expert in static electricity and flammable liquids. He did training and safety inspections for the company. One day an

Joe Boxmeyer giving one of his "fiery" presentations

acquaintance of his who happened to be a missionary aviator asked Joe if he had ever heard of Mission Safety International. He had not, but was fascinated by the fact that missions were interested in safety—a subject close to his heart. He contacted us at MSI, and before long we had Joe traveling the world with us from Africa to South America to the Pacific Rim. Joe's *explosive, fiery* presentations were such that they would *ignite* rapt attention—especially when he immersed a spark plug into a container of aviation gasoline! He loved missions and loved getting to know the missionaries. Venues for his demos on this trip varied from living rooms of homes to church auditoriums to classrooms and hangars.

Terry Moose probably traveled more with me than any other. He had retired from American Airlines as a 747 captain and had a heart for missionary aviation safety. Terry was also a trained counselor. He was instrumental in

Captain Terry Moose presenting at MSI seminar

developing the questions MSI used for doing our safety audit interviews—along with Merrill Piper and the Wycliffe Bible Translators personnel department. Often, his wife Mary would travel with him on our trips. She was a real trooper and often helped out in preparing reports of our survey results.

PNG is a really good place to experience "pork barbeque excellence" as in put the meat and vegetables in the ground over hot coals, cover, cook to perfection, and then enjoy. In PNG it's called a Mumu.

Preparing the Mumu food

Enjoying the Mumu food

PNG Mumu in the ground being cooked

Most Challenging and Frustrating Trip

The country and mission shall remain un-named. The purpose of the trip was to do a safety survey (now called audit) for a particular group. The flight program was well established, as it had been in operation for many years. The MSI team began our interviews, during which, through the course of two to three hour sessions and about 40 questions, it became painfully obvious that there was a problem. It didn't matter what question we asked. The answer almost immediately came back to—and focused on—one issue. This issue had been dominant on the program for a long time and continued to fester. That's all the interviewees wanted to talk about. It was obvious to the MSI team that the issue was affecting safety since attitudes and motivations of the staff were adversely affected.

At completion of our project we gave the mission administrators our written report which frankly laid out our findings and recommendations. The report was accepted with no apparent pushback at the time. However, some months later I received word indirectly that the mission was spreading the word that MSI had gone into the program and stirred up a hornet's nest by bringing up the issue they had long ago dealt with and put to rest. The disappointing thing was that they didn't bother to tell us but chose to spread the word to others instead.

Redemption finally came a year or two later when one of the mission officials told me that MSI was right—there had been a problem needing their attention after all. Unfortunately, there was no evidence that they did anything to correct the misinformation they had spread earlier to others.

Most Colorful Trips

Shells, plants and brightly colored paint are the ingredients of choice for these tribal villagers in Papua New Guinea to adorn their bodies for the huge "Goroka Show." They come from far and wide to the city of Goroka in the PNG highlands for the event. They strut their stuff through dances, shouts, and other maneuvers for the spectacular show. It lasts for several days. I had the privilege of attending during one of my visits to the country. There is an admission fee but also an extra fee if

At the PNG Goroka Show: all dressed up!

you bring in a camera—obviously some good business heads at work here!

Goroka Show participant

Next door, on the other half of the island is Papua, Indonesia. Papua, at my first recollection, was called Dutch New Guinea. After Indonesia took possession, it became known as West Irian, then Irian Jaya. Now it's called Papua. Papua is probably ten to twenty years behind PNG in development but, like their counterparts across the border, some like to dress up and show off. During one of my visits to the Regions Beyond Missionary Union (RBMU) aviation base in Taiveye, a village located in the lowlands, some of the locals knew I had a video camera so they dressed up for me. Some of the men put on a mock fight with their bows and arrows. One old guy had on a weird looking antique style football helmet he had obtained from somewhere, which was a stark contrast to his penis gourd that the men routinely wore. Ladies, of course, were decked out only in their Sunday-go-to-meeting grass skirts.

After the video session they all gathered around the mission house porch in the evening to see what I had captured of their antics. We were able to play the video from my camera onto a small TV that belonged to the missionary.

While there, I took video of a woman being treated for a snake bite. Death adders were common in the area, and she had been bitten on the foot. Treatment consisted of using an electric shock from a device similar to a cattle prod. It was believed the electric current could neutralize the venom. This is not so novel a concept in missionary circles. JAARS used to build and sell devices for this purpose. Last report I had at the time, the woman was doing well.

Speaking of colorful, on the other side of the world in several African countries we visited, the ladies wore beautiful brightly colored dresses and wraps. The reds and yellows really stood out. In a couple of countries the men wore white robes, along with a brightly colored sash and perhaps a turban, which made us Americans stand out as touristy and perhaps weird.

Colorful, in a sense other than bright colors, was a tribal war I witnessed in PNG. Seems there are always turf wars going on there as fights erupt over land disputes. This one took place literally next door to the New Tribes Mission (NTM) base just outside of Goroka. What I saw first was comical in a sense in that a guy pulled up in his Toyota pickup truck, parked, got out, retrieved his bow and arrows from the bed of the truck and headed across the highway to join the fight. I saw guys scattered along the hillside in tall grass shooting arrows at each other. Occasionally, one got hit by an arrow and someone took him next door to the mission base for treatment by the missionary medical personnel! After several hours, they seemed to tire of battle and gave it up to fight another day.

Generosity

Before I confess on my own, I will use my kids as an illustration. I have a son that I always said if he had a nickel he would rather give it away than carry it around in his pocket. I have a daughter who was a saver. Any money that came into her possession wasn't likely to go away any time soon. On the other hand, my other daughter was somewhere in between. Sometimes I wondered if she even knew if she had any money or not. Okay, I'm exaggerating a bit. I have never been a big spender and tried to weigh my options carefully, always looking for the best deal. My wife felt I was often too tight. She was a generous, giving person and taught me a lot by example over the years.

Where are you going with this, Joe?

In the early days of MSI's ministry, Terry Moose, one of MSI's founders and retired American Airlines captain, was usually with me as part of our team on our trips. After doing a safety seminar or audit, Terry would often offer to take our hosts out to dinner at a nice restaurant. This could typically be up to 20 people or so. It was a nice gesture, and they much appreciated it. Terry felt it was a special blessing to him personally.

Even though I was not on a retired airline captain's financial status by any means, in later years when Terry was not along, I sometimes felt the Lord had blessed me to the extent that I could offer to treat the mission folks we were ministering to in the same way. I always paid for the meals personally, since I did not feel comfortable using MSI funds for this purpose. After all, our agreement with the missions was that when we went out to do a seminar and/or audit, we would get ourselves there, but they were expected to take care of our local expenses of meals, housing and local transportation.

On one trip, as I was approaching retirement, the Lord laid on my heart a different project. This particular program in Africa had quite a few national workers. I knew they did not have much income and struggled financially. I wanted to help them in some way. In consultation with, and with the approval of the mission administration, we went to the local grocery store and bought foods and household supplies that I knew the recipients could take home to their families—flour, sugar, rice, and other things they could enjoy. At checkout, we asked the store clerks to divide the items into separate bags for us so all the bags had the same items.

Later, back at the hangar, as we gave out the bags to each individual, the expressions of gratitude on their faces were obvious. They had gratitude, but I was the one receiving the bigger blessing. I don't remember the exact cost, but think I spent a little over three hundred dollars at the grocery store.

But guess what. You can't out give God, right? Not too long after returning home from that trip, I received in the mail a notice from the Social Security Administration stating that my retirement benefits had been recalculated and that about another three hundred dollars was being deposited into my bank account! How about that, sports fans! It's fun to see how the Lord works.

Joe distributing gift packs to mission workers

Most Traumatic Trip

The year was 1993. We were on an extensive trip doing seminars and audits in several countries in Africa. We had been in Nairobi, Kenya first and then Dodoma, Tanzania for safety seminars. Speakers, in addition to me, were Dwight McSmith, Terry Moose, Robert Roper, and David Staveley. It was in Dodoma that Robert Roper (a pilot and professional fireman) had everyone gather on the hangar ramp in order to demonstrate the proper use of a fire extinguisher. After he talked about things such as staying upwind of the fire and swinging the extinguisher side to side in a sweeping motion aimed at the base of the fire, a large drip pan with gasoline was ignited for the demonstration. Robert then pulled the pin and pulled the trigger. Nothing! The extinguisher failed to work. We found out a bit latter that their procedure for checking the extinguishers in the hangar was to pull the trigger for a split second to verify that it would dispense material. That's a big no-no because the powder will eventually clog the valve and block any powder discharge. That is exactly what had happened. Lesson learned—dramatically! Never pull the trigger to test. Instead, check the pressure gage.

After the seminar in Dodoma, we made a stop in Mwanza, Tanzania where we were to be flown to Uganda in the MAF airplane. This was a brief stop, but we got to see the house where Jon Egeler, who took my place as MSI president in 2004, lived while serving as pilot/mechanic with AIM-AIR. They were not at home, because Jon and Pam needed to go to Nairobi for her to give birth.

The flight from Mwanza, Tanzania to Entebbe, Uganda in the MAF Cessna 206 was uneventful but interesting as we traveled northbound just to the west of Lake Victoria. After landing at Entebbe, we cleared immigration and customs formalities and were met by one of the MAF pilots serving there. He took me aside and informed me that they had received a message that my mother had died and that I should call dad in North Carolina. We still had to drive to the town of Kampala where the MAF base was located. After arriving in Kampala, the pilot took me to the MAF office to use their phone for calling dad. My mind was racing. Here we were in the middle of our trip. What do I do? Fortunately, I was able to get through to dad via telephone right away. The family had already discussed it, and they thought I should stay in Africa and finish the job rather than trying to get back home for the funeral. They would arrange to have the service video recorded. Torn between the options, I soon realized that they were right, but it was going to be tough. It helped that shortly before the trip, I had been with mom and dad and we had discussed the possibility that, due to mom's poor health, something like this might happen, and that they desired I not feel pressure to return. With the Lord's help, I stayed on. We finished the audit work in Uganda and then went to Nairobi, Kenya for the next seminar and audit before returning home—two weeks after the death of my mother. Ed and Dottie Essick met us in Nairobi to assist with the audit there. It wasn't easy being away from the family at that time but things went well overall. The love exhibited by the MSI team and the missionaries was a real comfort.

After returning back home to Tennessee in early March, I drove from Tennessee to North Carolina to spend a few days with dad. The Lord insisted I stay several days longer than planned by allowing "Superstorm '93" to dump up to three feet of snow over the whole area. I had to wait until snow was cleared and downed trees were removed from the highways over the mountains before I could get back home.

A Medical Challenge

The MSI team was scheduled to travel to Papua New Guinea (PNG) for a safety audit for MAF Australia (AMAF) which operated the flight program in PNG. The plan was to visit the AMAF headquarters in Melbourne, Australia, for interviews there first, then proceed to PNG and then, on the return, re-visit the headquarters in Melbourne and present our report. The team consisted of Harold Berk, Terry Moose and me. Tickets were bought and schedules made. We would rendezvous in Sydney, Australia and proceed together to Melbourne.

Several weeks before the trip, I began to experience pain, nausea and discomfort in my gut area. I had gone over to North Carolina for a safety visit to the Piedmont Bible College aviation program (Missionary Aviation Institute-MAI) and a visit to my parents. On the return home, late at night and passing through Boone, NC, I experienced such pain and nausea that I had to pull over into a parking lot and stop. After ten or so minutes, I was able to continue home the remaining hour. Time to see a doctor. My primary physician diagnosed it as a gall bladder problem and referred me to a surgeon who said I needed surgery right away. "But I have an important trip in several weeks to PNG. Will I be still able to make the trip?" He thought I probably could, and surgery was scheduled. They found the gall bladder to be so hardened that it was too risky to use the laparoscopic procedure, so I got the eight inch cut. Things were worse than they thought. I had developed septicemia and other complications and ended up staying in the hospital eight days. Dr. Martin, who was from the Philippines, was the surgeon—a good, but no-nonsense guy. When he came in to take my drain tube out after a couple of days, his only words were, "Hold your horses." He braced his knee against the side of the bed and gave the tube a yank!

On my follow-up visit to Dr. Martin's office, I asked if it was still okay for me to make my trip. "Well, I don't know about that, Joe. It's a long trip, and you probably will be a long ways from good medical care if an issue comes up—but send me a postcard!" I bought a postcard in PNG with a picture of one of the natives decked out in feathers and paint and sent it to him with a note saying I had found me another doctor!

I had told Harold and Terry to go ahead with their plans and that they should do the initial Melbourne visit without me. I would come later and meet them in Sydney, where we would continue our trip to PNG. I talked to Qantas Airlines about the ticket schedule change. Yes, they could reschedule, but I would have to pay the new current, higher fare. Even with a letter from the doctor. Bummer.

In all my travels spanning over forty years and forty countries, I never experienced any serious issues other than a delayed bag. Until now. Here's how it went down. After departing Tri-City airport in Tennessee for the next stop in Cincinnati, for some reason, I looked at my baggage claim tickets (which I hardly ever do) and saw that they showed my bags were to be placed on the New Guinea airline in Los Angeles instead of Sydney. They don't fly to Los Angeles! *Oh, groan, now I'll have to get this changed when I get to Cincinnati.* After arrival, I went to the ticket counter and explained the situation. They said they would have to try to find my bags, put them on the belt at baggage claim, where I would have to retrieve them and bring them to the counter for rechecking. Now, the doctor had given me strict orders to not lift anything over fifteen pounds. Baggage claim was downstairs. The bags showed up. Now I had to lug them back upstairs to the check-in counter. Fortunately, I found an elevator. This time, they were correctly routed and checked all the way to PNG. That done, I continued on to Los Angeles (LAX) for the Qantas flight scheduled for 9:00 p.m.

Now seated on the Boeing 747-400 plane at LAX for the 15 hour flight to Sydney, and time for departure, the captain made the announcement that our departure would be delayed since fog had rolled in over the airport from the Pacific Ocean. About an hour later, the captain announced that the fog had dispersed slightly and they were going to give it a try—all we have to do is find the runway first, he said. After about 15 minutes of taxiing, the end of the runway was at hand, but now the captain said the fog had worsened and that we would have to go back to the terminal. Returning to the gate, we sat for a while longer and then came the announcement that the flight had been cancelled. We needed to collect our bags at baggage claim, board a bus and be taken to a hotel for the night. Oh, groan. More lugging of luggage. I got the bags onto the bus and off again at the hotel, got checked in and lugged the bags to the room. Next morning, the process reversed, and the bags were once again deposited with the agent at the check-in counter. The one trip in my lifetime during which I was restricted physically, became the most demanding. Go figure!

I arrived in Sydney where I met up with Harold and Terry almost a day late. We continued to PNG on Air Niugini and were met in Mt. Hagen by the AMAF personnel. I felt every bump in the road on the ride from the airport to our accommodations. We were in PNG two weeks doing the audit and then returned to AMAF headquarters in Melbourne to debrief and give them our written report. The pain lessened and I felt almost completely healed by the time I arrived back home in Tennessee.

Floating Along

Effervescent is a good word to describe Brian Pill. Brian was the MAF pilot flying the Cessna 185 on straight floats that was based in Uganda. The MSI team was there to do a safety audit of the aviation program and part of our evaluation was to fly with the pilots to observe their operations. Brian had a flight to a couple of the islands of Lake Victoria so this was a good opportunity for me to ride along. The first leg involved delivering a Ugandan pastor and his wife to their home. The second leg was to another island to deliver medical supplies to a nurse based there and to check on the pastor and his family.

Floatplane dock with canal leading to Lake Victoria in background

The floatplane base was unique in that MAF had a water channel dug about a kilometer long that connected Lake Victoria to their airport. It was just deep enough and wide enough to taxi the airplane back and forth and was located adjacent to the end of the wheel plane airstrip.

After a slight delay while MAF mechanic Stan Lincoln repaired a broken wire to the fuel pump, Brian pumped the floats and we loaded up. Taxiing along the channel, we arrived at the lake and departed. It was a bone-jarring takeoff due to choppiness of the water but soon we were airborne and on our way. Off to the right I could see the east-west runway of the Entebbe airport. This brought back memories of the events described in the book *Raid on Entebbe* telling of the daring night landing in 1976 when the Israelis came in to rescue their people who had been taken hostage. When we arrived in Entebbe a few days earlier, we saw the bullet holes still visible in the old terminal building.

Landing at our first island destination, Brian got out, turned the plane around by hand, and pushed it backward onto the beautiful, white sand beach. Then, one of the most impressive acts of servanthood I have seen. There is a problem in those waters with a little parasitic worm carried by a snail that can burrow into the body and cause a condition called bilharzia. It is treatable but can be very serious. Brian waded over to the float and had the pastor's wife get on his back. Then he carried her the few feet to shore so she didn't have to get in the water and risk getting the disease.

Pilot helping pastor's wife from float plane to shore

Departing, after a brief visit, we arrived at the tiny island which was to be our next stop. Nearly the whole town came out to greet us—all fifty or so of them. With giggly, smiling kids hanging on to us, we walked about a hundred yards to the "village," which consisted of mere

Joe in village on Lake Victoria

shacks of wood and plastic. We delivered the medical supplies to the nurse who ran the small clinic there, and paid a short visit to encourage the local pastor and his family.

We said our goodbyes, untied the ropes and made the short flight back to the mouth of the channel. We had no passengers, so Brian allowed me the honor of making the landing. I had minimal float time but a lot of Cessna 185 time so it worked acceptably well. Brian took over for the taxi back up the channel. Oops! Even with a touch of power the plane came to a halt. We had hit bottom in the narrow, shallow channel. He wouldn't let me get out to help due to the bilharzia risk, but two guys "happened" to be close by and came to help. They pulled down on the tail while Brian gunned the engine and we broke free. Thus,

my fantastic float plane experience on Lake Victoria came
to an end.

Safety Survey/Audit Explained

Originally, what we call an audit today was called a survey. This was due to the fact that the word audit conjured up thoughts of an unfriendly, undesired process. The survey consists of a series of about forty interview questions that we ask of all the personnel involved in the aviation operation. That can be all the way from top administrators, managers, mechanics, pilots, to hangar helpers, flight dispatchers and secretaries. The questions were carefully developed by Merrill Piper who was JAARS Director of Aviation Safety, Captain Terry Moose who was with American Airlines but worked a lot with missionary aviation groups in various ways, and the counselling department of Wycliffe. The questions were so professionally designed, and worked so well over the years, that we dared not mess with them any more than to adapt to more current conditions. They were originally developed for JAARS but when I started MSI, I contacted Merrill and he graciously shared their use with us.

We tell the folks that the interview will probably take anywhere from two to four hours. Two, if the person is of few words, and gives brief answers. Four, if the person is the talkative type and goes on and on in response to each question. We block out four hours for the interview because we want the interviewees to have all the time necessary to express their feelings. The person being interviewed is assured up front that nothing he or she says will be associated with them in our report. Their responses are treated as confidential within the MSI team.

The questions are designed in such a way as to bring out a person's true feelings about the topic. Sometimes, a later question will approach the same topic from a different direction to more fully explore the issue.

At the end of each day, the team gets together to discuss the findings of the day and see if there are specific items that need follow-up or if significant issues are showing up.

In addition to the interviews, the team does inspections of the hangar, shops, and other facilities, and the aircraft. We ride with the pilots on flights as an observer to see how they perform and react to real-world situations as they develop—such as weather changes, airstrip conditions, and uncooperative passengers or officials. These are what I call the "killer" items. They tell me about the person's decision-making and judgment much better than just going out and observing how he does with slow-flight, stalls, and short-field landings.

After the interviews, flights, and inspections are completed, the team pools the information and formulates a written report. The report contains an executive summary, findings of any critical safety items, commendations, and recommendations for improvement. The report is first presented in draft form to the administration/management personnel to make sure we haven't misinterpreted a situation or need to give additional clarification. Then, we encourage the mission to share the report with the entire group to give them an opportunity to "cuss" and "discuss" with us. We believe that those who have participated in the interviews and shared their information have a right to know the results—all to the betterment and safety of the organization. Overall, we have found the missionary aviation community to be very open, honest and willing to share. After all, these attributes are what it takes to have a successful, effective team and a safe operation.

Catching People Doing What Is Right

Going into an audit, we like to point out what the folks are doing right. This draws attention to the act or situation, reinforces it and hopefully results in it being continued. We all like to be complimented. In the audit report we actually list things that we find commendable.

Here are some examples. A clean aircraft usually means other details are cared for as well. We like to find that all aircraft maintenance work is well documented and

Well organized tool box - a place for every tool

done in a timely manner. The same goes for an orderly, neat hangar and office. We compliment good signage such as "No Smoking," fire extinguisher locations, passenger waiting areas, and exits. When tool storage boards are shadowed with the outline of the tool that belongs there, and tool box drawers have designated places for each tool, this will surely be pointed out in the report as this helps insure that tools are not inadvertently left in the aircraft after maintenance.

We are quick to point out the good work done on airstrips that are well marked, fenced, grass kept regularly mowed and the approach/departure zones clear of obstacles. Our hearts are warmed when we observe good safety equipment and practices—grinding wheels with guards in place and located well away from any flammable substances, S-frame crashworthy seats in the aircraft, pilots wearing helmets, standardized instrument panels, etc. On one of my early visits to Irian Jaya I was so impressed with Dave Ketchum's attire that I had to take his picture. He was

Pilot dressed for safety

dressed in helmet, Nomex (fire resistant) flight suit and gloves.

"S" frame seat designed for progressive collapse in crash to reduce G load on occupant

The S-frame seat design is an outgrowth of the NASA aircraft crash tests done at Langley Field in Virginia. NASA found that in most airplane crashes the vertical loads are typically higher than the horizontal. The S-frame seat was designed to progressively collapse and thus reduce g-loads on the occupant of the seat. JAARS played a huge role in the final design and getting the seat into production. They are now installed in many missionary aircraft around the world.

It was also found that the double strap shoulder harness was much more effective than the single strap. Some missions only had them installed for the front seat occupants but MSI strongly recommends they be available for all occupants.

NASA crash testing at Langley Field in Virginia

Other commendable items we love to be able to include in our report are such things as good passenger briefings before flight, staff working together well (teamwork), well planned and executed pilot/mechanic checking and training, proper handling of hazardous cargo (i.e. dangerous goods), and good security and lighting of

Joe with NASA crash-tested airplane

the facilities. This list is not comprehensive by any means, just a representative sample.

What Could Go Wrong... Go Wrong... Go Wrong...

Even the best-run programs will usually have several areas we can identify as needing correction, change, or adding for maximum safety and efficiency. We identify these and give recommendations for improvement. Over the years, "We've seen it all," as the saying goes. Following are some examples.

Sometimes, air pressure is used to pump fuel from drums. It takes very few pounds-per-square-inch (PSI) of pressure. We have seen bulging drums as a result of over-

Bulging fuel drum

Broken pressure gage

pressurization due to carelessness or the fact that the pressure gage was broken.

Disorganization and clutter are two areas we often find in need of improvement. It may take the form of liquids stored in unmarked containers, drums of oil, avgas and/or jet fuel stored side by side and without distinguishable labeling, fire extinguishers placed on the floor rather than mounted at the prescribed height, oily rags left lying around, or damaged electric cords, uncovered electric outlets and unlabeled circuit breakers. In one hangar there were so many cords and air hoses strung out across the floor and aircraft parts and workbenches in the way, one could hardly navigate from one area to the other without bumping into or tripping over something.

Hangar floor clutter noted during safety inspection

It was not unusual to find a spark-generating grinding wheel or battery charger located close to a solvent parts cleaning area or other flammable liquid. Joe Boxmeyer, our flammable materials and static electricity expert, was keen on thoroughly checking for proper bonding when handling flammable liquids such as during fueling and defueling aircraft.

Bonding is the act of connecting two parts together, usually via a wire, so that both parts are at the same electrical equivalent. Since both parts are at the same electrical level there can be no spark from one to the other. For example, it is desired that the fueling nozzle be bonded to the aircraft airframe at or near the fuel tank opening so that if they touch no spark will be generated. This is more important than grounding, which simply means that the part is connected electrically to the ground. Often, the person fueling the aircraft would connect the bonding wire to the exhaust stack of the aircraft engine or nose wheel steering bolt, which did not provide adequate bonding.

Joe, with his ohmmeter, showed that there was not always a bond to the airframe due to corrosion, grease or exhaust gaskets. Better to connect the bonding (grounding) wire to a place near the fueling port such as the wing tie down ring. On one base we found the fueling equipment grounding wire connected to a metal grate in the concrete ramp. The problem was that the grate was merely resting in the concrete channel and not making any contact with the earth!

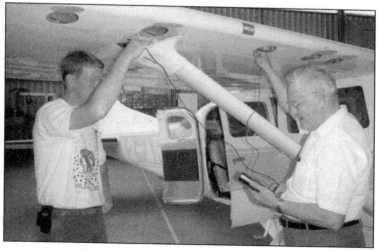

Joe Boxmeyer testing for good bonding point

Rickety ladders, or those of improper height, are not uncommon findings. There have been serious falls with injury as a result. Sometimes the person just doesn't want to take time to get the proper ladder from across the way or it may be there is a reluctance to spend the money required for a new one.

Hazards to the program are not always manifest in the physical "unsafe <u>condition</u>" arena. There's also the "unsafe <u>acts</u>" that must be dealt with. (Actually, studies show that unsafe conditions only account for about 20% of the problem, whereas, unsafe acts account for about 80%.) This can be the result of many factors. Possibly there is an inter-personal conflict or a resistance to authority. Perhaps a manager is putting too much pressure on those answerable to him. Pressure can be in many forms. For example, bending the rules to get the job done; taking a flight when the weather is questionable; overloading the aircraft; working extra hours or coming to work when fatigued or not feeling well.

These are just a few examples of the types of problems we are apt to find during the safety audit inspection. Our job is to uncover such problems and make recommendations (with follow-up) for proper solutions. Our professional staff and volunteers, along with our tried and true interview process, helps us accomplish that in a relatively short time.

Safety Efforts from the Past

Some panned out, others not so much.

In addition to the S-frame seat development and widespread use of shoulder harnesses, other things have been tried in an effort to increase missionary aviation safety. Many of the ideas implemented or experimented with were the results of property damage, injury or even death in missionary aviation accidents. Here are some

Showing additional vernier control for alternate fuel system

examples. Nate Saint, while flying in Ecuador in the early 1950s, developed a rudimentary alternate fuel system whereby fuel was injected directly into the carburetor air inlet venturi thus bypassing trouble prone areas such as the fuel valve, fuel filter and carburetor interior parts. Over the years it was refined and adapted for use in the Cessnas including those with fuel injection systems rather than carburetors. It was used for many years and provided some "saves" after engine power loss, but its use was eventually discontinued due to other risks it introduced in addition to the high level of proficiency required for its safe use.

For tailwheel-type airplanes, a device called a rake brake was developed which, when activated in the cockpit, would drop down and rotate back underneath the tailwheel and dig into the ground. This would help stop the airplane when braking was ineffective due to brake failure or slippery airstrips. It proved to be effective, but for obvious reasons would only work with tailwheel type airplanes.

Rake brake stowed

Rake brake deployed

Other airframe modifications were experimented with for occupant protection but proved to be impractical due to cost or difficulty of retrofit. One modification involved installing skid tubing from under the engine back to the bottom of the cabin firewall. It was found that in some nose-low crashes, the firewall area of the airframe would dig into the ground contributing to high g-loads or flipping the plane over.

Another modification involved installing a steel tubing cage inside the cockpit area to prevent the structure from collapsing onto the occupants in a crash. Yet another modification was to install quick disconnects in the fuel lines that would separate and seal during a crash.

Steel cockpit cage modification in progress

Picture illustrating the need for better occupant protection

Short Field Take-off and Landing (STOL) kits have been installed on many missionary airplanes over the years. Note, in the photo below, the four white stall fences on top of the wing.

Probably the most effective, and expensive, is the Robertson kit which adds a drooped wing leading edge, stall fences and ailerons interconnected with the wing flaps so the ailerons go down some when the flaps are extended.

Another was the Wren, which had similar features (and even more expensive) but added a canard which is similar to the horizontal tail but was mounted near the front

Wren aircraft modification showing canard at front of airplane and stall fences on top of wing

of the aircraft. There were (and still are) other modification kits such as the Owl and Horton. Not long after these aftermarket kits began to come onto the scene, Cessna started adding only the leading edge cuff to some of their factory models.

Speculator Seaplane Seminar

Moody Aviation had been providing a speaker to the seaplane pilot annual fly-in held at Camp of the Woods in Speculator, NY for several years. Usually, they would show a Moody Institute of Science film or something similar. After MSI came into existence, the Moody Aviation Director, Ken Simmelink, came to me and said

Seaplanes on beach at Camp-of-the-Woods, Speculator NY

that since we were in the business of doing seminars, perhaps we should take over the seaplane seminar. I agreed. For several years, until they stopped holding the fly-in there, MSI provided a speaker for their safety seminar (overseen by the Albany FAA office) and also handled the Sunday service included in their program.

More often than not, the special speakers we brought in would do a safety seminar presentation and also be the Sunday service speaker. For example, Craig Gahagen was the speaker one year and talked about his float flying experiences in Peru with the South America Mission Aviation (SAMAIR) program, and then on Sunday talked about the spiritual aspects of their ministry in Peru through the use of the airplane. Of course, we had Dwight McSmith there to talk about the NASA crash testing program, and others. One of the others was Tom Hamilton who was in the process of developing the Kodiak airplane specifically for missionary aviation. Tom gave some good insights into the new airplane's development.

Gordon Purdy was the director at Camp of the Woods at the time. He was a pilot, so when approached by the Seaplane Pilots Association (SPA) about holding their fly-in at the camp facility, Gordon said yes, but only with the condition that they include a Sunday service as part of their program. They had excellent housing, food, conference room, a dock, and a beautiful beach for parking the seaplanes. As I mentioned earlier, the FAA ran the safety seminar part of the fly-in. I often gave seminar presentations and sometimes spoke at the Sunday service if a guest speaker was not available.

Joe & Elaine Hopkins & Craig & Heather Gahagen at a seaplane seminar in Speculator, New York

Oshkosh- EAA Airventure

In the late 1980s, MAF put out a notice to their alumni that they were looking for volunteers to help with their booth at the Experimental Aircraft Association (EAA) annual fly-in held in Oshkosh, WI. I contacted them with an offer saying I would love to help them if they would allow me to promote MSI "under the table", that is, I would represent MAF with the understanding that if anyone asked about MSI, I could give them my brochure and answer any questions. This worked well for a couple of years. EAA did not allow booth sharing, so groups were not allowed to go

Joe & Elaine representing MAF - 1991

in together for a spot. However, a work-around was developed. International Association of Missionary Aviation (IAMA) could have a booth (a tent in this case) and allow their members to have their own tables.

At first, the tent was a rather small, silver canvas tent. It was dark and uninviting inside unless the sides could be opened—which was a problem with wind or when it rained. Later, IAMA was able to arrange for a much larger, white tent which allowed in more light and worked out great. We had our own MSI table until a few years ago when our space was relinquished to allow another mission

Early tent used by mission aviation at Oshkosh fly-in

to come in. MSI then, took over manning of the Hospitality Tent which was adjacent and provided tables, chairs and refreshments where visitors and other contacts could have a more private area to talk with MSI and other mission representatives.

Aviation people come to EAA in Oshkosh from all over the world. Over 600,000 persons typically attend each year. It is the premier aviation event. Over 10,000 aircraft

Bigger & better tent for mission aviation at Oshkosh fly-in

of every description fly in. Everything from ultralight, to home built, to antique, to corporate, to military,—and even airline types. Every aviation vendor one can imagine is represented. In addition to the incredible aerobatic performances and warbird fly-overs, there are workshops for such things as welding and fabric covering. There are forums every day covering a multitude of topics. I made forum safety presentations on three different occasions over the years and was interviewed by EAA for their *Timeless Voices* program which is available for listening to this day on their website. EAA's latest figures state that for the year 2021 there were over 1,000 forums, workshops and presentations during the week. All of this provides a rich source of information and resources for missionary aviators, recruiters, and those who want to know more

Joe Hopkins presenting at EAA Oshkosh forum

about missionary aviation. In fact, many students apply for training at the schools, and new candidates decide to sign up with a mission as a result of the contacts made at EAA.

A local non-profit group called Missionary Aviation Support Association (MASA) sets up a tent in the camping area and provides meals, housing and loaner vehicles for the missionaries in attendance. They also arrange for them to speak in the area churches and do radio interviews. MASA has been doing this for many years without cost to the missionaries, and this service continues to the present.

MASA had its small beginnings in the early 1970's but took on exponential growth starting in 1990 when Lee and Debbie Smoll became involved and enlisted the help of local churches and volunteers. As of this writing, MASA serves an average of 225 missionaries each year.

Meal tent - 1991

Meal tent - 2014

ISASI / SERC, ETC.

I first joined the International Society of Air Safety Investigators (ISASI), in 1971 right after completing the Accident Investigation & Prevention course at the University of California. Since then, I have attended several of their annual safety conferences. More recently, the ISASI Southeast Region Chapter (SERC) became active and started holding their own conferences. I had the privilege of being a presenter at three of those—one in Cocoa Beach, FL in 2014, one in Pensacola, FL in 2015, and most recently in Savannah, GA in 2016.

Joe Hopkins presenting at SERC, Pensacola FL

My presentations were, of course, safety related. I used missionary aviation operations and accidents as the basis of my talks. In addition to giving out, I also took in, learning information from the other presenters that I could use for MSI's benefit. Networking also happens at these events. We make contacts for our mailing list who sometimes will become financial supporters, and occasionally may find a fellow believer interested in volunteering his or her services to MSI.

Smoking or Non-smoking?

In the 1970s when I first started attending industry safety conferences, smoking was allowed (and common) in the conference room. Also, smoking was permitted on airline flights although usually confined to a designated area in the rear of the cabin. It was no fun to come home from a conference or airline flight with clothes smelling like the inside of an ashtray. Thankfully, as the years passed, smoking was no longer allowed in conference rooms or on the airlines. However, before that changed, it seems I would often get assigned an airline seat one or two rows in front of the smoking section—might as well have been in the section itself for all the good it did, being that close. Also, think of the poor non-smoker pilot assigned to fly with a smoker pilot. The wheels of progress turn slowly, they say, but eventually this issue went away— domestically in the 1990s and internationally by about 2000.

Longevity pays—if you do it safely

Well, it doesn't always pay in financial terms, but sometimes by way of recognition of special accomplishment. As I think back on my years of flying and some of the experiences I wrote of earlier in this book, I wonder how I survived—except for the grace of God. In 2010 I was given the Wright Brothers Master Pilot Award by the Department of

Transportation, Federal Aviation Administration (FAA) for fifty years of accident free flying. The FAA chose the Tennessee Aviation Hall of Fame Museum in Sevierville for the award presentation. Along with the plaque came a certificate and lapel pin. They even gave my wife a special certificate and lapel pin as well.

Related to this is an article in the August 2011 AOPA PILOT magazine. It was written by Kathy Dondzilla and recounted some of my experiences as a missionary pilot and safety guy. At the conclusion of the article she pointed out that I was recipient of the Wright Brothers Master Pilot Award and added that although I am now a Master Pilot, I had always been "the Master's" pilot.

Hopkins presented with Wright Brothers Master Pilot Award - 2010

Security

It was probably in the late 1980s, when email was just coming into being, that I got word from Moody Aviation that they had received an email message from a missionary pilot in Colombia that was to be passed on to me. The message, from Al Meehan, said he was interested in becoming involved in the MSI ministry upon his return to the USA. Al was with JAARS where he served as pilot/mechanic and field administrator.

Sometime after that, when he returned to the USA, we got together and worked out an arrangement for him to help us with the seminars and audits. Al had a special interest in the security aspects of safety. Because of that, MSI utilized his talents and expertise throughout ensuing seminars and audits. After settling back into stateside life, he worked part-time for the local sheriff department as a deputy in addition to his duties with JAARS and MSI. Al went with us on many trips. His seminar talks usually centered around topics such as avoiding becoming a hostage, or how to act if you are one, securing your home, and being alert while in your vehicle or other means of transportation. During the audits, he looked at hangar security, lighting, fire safety, and other things such as making sure one's safe is bolted to the floor or wall. While he was with us on a trip to Botswana, a case in point (see photo) emerged. One of the staff houses was broken into during the night while two missionary ladies were sleeping. Several items were stolen from the living room. The windows had bars but the burglars cut and pried them out of the way to gain entry.

Home invasion by cutting bars on window

He always insisted that in our MSI documents and communications, we mentioned not only safety but security as well. Al continues to be a valuable resource today.

A Dream Trip

At last count in 2021, I have touched down in 49 countries and spent time in 42. Several years ago I envisioned my MSI traveling days being reduced or potentially ending, and realized I had not yet been to Ecuador. I said to myself, "Self, you have to go to Ecuador where so much of the early history of missionary aviation took place." It was a short conversation, and I began to plan how to make it happen.

Ecuador was the country where Nate Saint, one of MAF's first pilots, was assigned. He and four other missionaries were killed there in 1956 by the Auca Indians during their attempt to befriend them and reach them with the Gospel—an event that shocked the world and caused many to dedicate their lives to missionary service.

I contacted Dan Whitehead, who was the MAF program manager in Ecuador. Dan and his wife Tracy had attended our church in Elizabethton, where he served as minister of music while a student at Moody Aviation. Also, MSI had provided a safety seminar for MAF in Venezuela while Dan was program manager there. I explained that although MSI was not scheduled for anything in Ecuador, I was bound and determined to visit on my own, but that I would be happy to help in any way I could while there. Dan responded by asking me to do a safety seminar for them.

He said they would also invite the local commercial and military aviation people to attend.

MSI seminar in Shell Mera, Ecuador, for missions and local aviation personnel

The seminar was well attended and well received. I enjoyed my visit with the MAFers there. It was especially good to see, and roam around in, the house Nate Saint built

House built by Nate Saint, MAF pilot, in Shell Mera

before his martyrdom, even though it was not occupied at the time and was in need of repairs. There was talk of tearing it down but fortunately that did not happen. Recognizing the historical value, the house was restored a few years later.

The visit exceeded my expectations. I was able to visit the actual area where Nate Saint and the other four missionaries gave their lives in an attempt to reach the Aucas with the Gospel. The river was up, so we could not identify any sandbars or possible location where the incident took place, but the locals took me to the edge of the Curaray River near where it all happened. Back in the village, I saw the marker erected in memory of Rachel Saint for her years of living among, and ministering to, the tribe.

Joe on bank of Cururay River in Ecuador near where 5 missionaries were martyred in 1956

Joe in front of monument in Shell Mera honoring Nate Saint

I was awed by seeing a large model of Nate's yellow airplane displayed high on a tower in a park in downtown Shell Mera commemorating his time of ministry there.

I asked the MAF staff there if they had seen evidence of the hydroelectric generator that Nate had built to provide electricity for the base. They had not, but thought it would be a fun adventure to see if we could find it. Several of us decked out with machetes, cameras, and knee-high rubber boots slipped and slid down the hillside through plants and brush to the stream below. We waded upstream and finally came across the remnants of a small concrete dam and waterway. Going back downstream while trying to see where the concrete waterway might lead, we started chopping the thick undergrowth with machetes. Clink. That was the sound of metal on metal. More machete chops, and there before us was what was left of a waterwheel. We found it! Additional chops revealed more of the generator location including a concrete water tank for directing the water over the waterwheel. My pictures provide great memories of that discovery to this day.

Joe beginning search for Nate Saint's water wheel

Water wheel exposed!

Parts of water wheel, generator and water pipe

Back in Quito for my return flight to the USA, I was given a tour of the city by MAF pilot Fred Schmidt. This included the opportunity to stand on the equator with one foot in the northern hemisphere and one foot in the southern hemisphere. (I had done this one other time in the country of Kalimantan on the other side of the world.) Also included was a visit to the facilities of the Christian broadcasting station HCJB which broadcasts the Gospel worldwide by way of shortwave.

Joe visited HCJB radio station headquarters

Joe at the equator in Quito, Ecuador

The Need for MSI

Joe Boxmeyer, MSI's volunteer flammable liquids and static electricity expert taught in his seminars that static electricity is generated by the separation of two dissimilar materials. Something as simple as running a comb through your hair can create a spark, as will walking across a carpet.

This truth was vividly demonstrated in Senegal a number of years ago during refueling of a Piper Aztec airplane. After adding fuel to the airplane tank, the pilot whipped out the dipstick he used to measure the amount of fuel in the tank from his back pocket. As he started to place the dipstick into the tank, it sparked over to the airframe and caught the fuel vapors on fire at the filler opening. Somehow, he was able to put the fire out with minimal damage, but it could have been more serious.

In another case, this time in Alaska, the pilot was draining fuel from the Bonanza airplane wing into a bucket. When he reached for the full bucket to replace it with an empty one, the charge developed on his body from walking across the hangar floor, sparked to the bucket and caught the fuel on fire. This resulted in major damage to the airplane before it could be extinguished.

Those are just two examples of how an MSI seminar can help educate missionary mechanics and pilots to the dangers and help prevent great losses to property and possibly life itself.

Other issues we deal with in our seminars, bulletins, and audit discussions are such things as falls, self-imposed pressure to make a flight, management pressure to make a flight, double inspections of maintenance work and developing, and abiding by, professional standards of operation. I remember a pilot telling me several years ago about being scheduled to make a flight but he felt he shouldn't do it because of the weather conditions. His program manager then said, "Well, if you are not willing to do it, I guess I'll have to." What a put down. Better if the manager had said something to the effect that he appreciated the pilot's concern and lower experience level, so he would take the flight instead.

A pilot had previously served a term on the field in PNG where he had experienced some significant stresses and now was back for a new term after a much-needed furlough. Shortly after arrival back on the field and caring for various items necessary for getting acclimated, he loaded his family and belongings into the mission aircraft for the flight to where he would be based. Weather was not good but he thought it was feasible. It was not. Trying to stay visual under a low ceiling of cloud just above the mountainous terrain, the aircraft slammed into the ground sending him and his family into eternity.

Overconfidence coupled with pressure to complete a flight, led to the demise of a pilot and his two passengers in Honduras. Overconfidence, because the pilot had flown in the country for many years and "knew the terrain like the back of his hand." He seldom even had a chart in the airplane with him. Pressure, because he had been on an overnight trip with a visitor from the USA who needed to catch an international flight back home. The flight should have taken only 20 minutes or so. Finding the mountain pass blocked, the pilot elected to climb above the cloud with the hope that he would find a hole to descend through at the destination. There was no hole there, so it is speculated that his plan was to continue another five or ten minutes to a large valley where he would typically find on opening in the cloud which would allow him to get under the cloud layer. It appears he started his descent toward the valley and down through the clouds too soon because the aircraft struck the side of a mountain and all three perished. Ironically, the crash site was within visual range of his home base.

Elmer Reaser was a longtime pilot with MAF who flew in Brazil and then later, as flight instructor in MAF's pre-field training program. Elmer became a longtime pilot with over 10,000 hours of safe flying because of his conservative, cautious approach to flying. As he often explained in his training and conversations, he believed in the principle that God could protect a snakebite victim overnight waiting for a flight in daylight or better weather, just easily as He could protect a stupid pilot who would succumb to the pressure of making poor flight decisions under the guise of needing to save a life.

Elmer also likened his piloting decisions to the game of baseball wherein, with three strikes, you are out. After strikes one or two, if things not looking good, one had better be seriously considering strong alternatives, rather than continuing on under the circumstances. This is the kind of decision making MSI looks to instill in all missionary aviation personnel through our seminars, audits, conversations and publications.

If you have read this far in the book, thank you. You have seen that I did not always make the best of decisions in my piloting career. However, God has seen fit to preserve my life. The formation of MSI is certainly a result. I am as surprised as anyone! I don't feel qualified to be the founder, but for some reason God had me in mind. I must acknowledge what I have heard from various sources, that God doesn't choose qualified people; He qualifies those He chooses. I'm humbled.

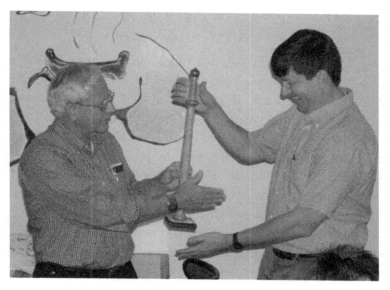

Transfer of control from Joe Hopkins to Jon Egeler

I'm grateful to have been given the privilege of continuing to serve on a part time basis with MSI after turning over the president/CEO position (control stick, if you will) to Jon Egeler in 2004. I've tried hard to not be the meddling founder that has plagued some organizations. It is easy for me as I acknowledge that MSI is not my organization—it is God's. To God be the glory!

The Personal Testimony of Joe Hopkins

I was blessed to have Christian parents who were true Christ-followers. I grew up in a Christian home and church environment. Because of this, I heard the good news early, of how we all are sinners and that Jesus Christ came to earth, was crucified and raised from the dead for my own sins. I accepted Him as my personal Savior at the age of nine. Thankfully, I was spared the problems and sinful ways so often encountered by those who don't hear about or come to know Jesus personally until later in life.

We had many missionaries speak in our church and visit in our home, so I knew there was a need for believers to go tell the good news to those who needed to hear about Jesus. Not all missionaries are preachers. Some serve in other ways such as the medical field. Since I had interests and skills in the technical area, I took training in the aviation field and served many years in missions as a pilot and mechanic. My family did this in Brazil, Honduras and later in the USA, where I trained future missionary pilots, first at the MAF base in California and then in Tennessee at Moody Aviation.

In 1983, I founded Mission Safety International (MSI) to help reduce accidents and save lives in missionary aviation. The Lord has blessed these efforts, and we believe that many lives have been saved both physically and spiritually.

I have lived over three-fourths of my expected life span and am here to tell you that living the life of a believer is the only way to go. God will bless you in ways hard to imagine, and provide for your needs as promised in Matthew 6:33, where we are encouraged to "seek first the kingdom of God and His righteousness and all these things (food, clothing, etc.) shall be added unto you."

I am so glad that becoming a believer is not complicated. The Bible tells us that if we believe in the Lord Jesus Christ and accept Him into our lives as personal Savior, we will have eternal life, that is, go to be with God when we die. "To be absent from the body is to be present with the Lord (1 Corinthians 5:8)." It does not get any better than that!

AOPA Pilot Article

Following is an early draft of an article for AOPA magazine written by Kathy Dondzilla. The final article was printed with a photo in AOPA Pilot magazine in August 2011 issue.

Joseph Guy Hopkins, Jr.

After Joe Hopkins delivered two missionaries to their Brazilian villages, he took off and headed back to home base. He had planned to follow the highway home, but he couldn't see it due to the low scud. Hopkins climbed to 7,000 feet and remembers, "I finally made the decision to just go on instruments." Knowing the area well, but with no VOR available he tuned the ADF to a broadcast radio station near his destination, hoping that when he arrived visibility would have improved enough to see the airport. He found his way and landed safely that day, but not without a sobering realization of the challenges pilots face flying in remote areas – the radio station was washed down the river a couple of weeks later in a flood! This knowledge would eventually help to refocus his life on improving aviation safety.

As a young man, Hopkins felt called to missionary work, and completed two programs at Moody Aviation – one in radio technology, and one in aviation. He soloed a Piper J-3 Cub in 1959, worked through a series of certificates and ratings, and graduated in 1962 with the following: commercial with instrument and certified flight instructor certificates, and an airframe and powerplant (A&P) license. After hundreds of landings in a variety of aircraft, he quips that undoubtedly, the best thing he landed at Moody was Elaine, a Registered Nurse, who eventually became his wife. Together they began work in the mission field through Mission Aviation Fellowship (MAF), which led them to Brazil. They served a couple of years, with Joe flying all over the rugged terrain before returning to the States to train missionary students in the rigors of bush and jungle flying. Hopkins later relocated to Tennessee to accept a position as flight instructor at Moody Aviation's missionary pilot training school.

The tragic deaths of a fellow pilot and a flight engineer in an aircraft accident renewed his resolve to improve aviation safety. Hopkins, himself, was supposed to have flown that aircraft that day, but the other pilot had replaced him at the last minute. He turned his grief into action and founded Mission Safety International (MSI) in 1983 to provide safety programs and services for aviation-based mission organizations and training institutes around the world. Since then, Hopkins has visited about 35 countries, providing safety seminars and operational audits to aviators serving in remote areas. A few years ago, he turned over the day-to-day operations of MSI to Jon Egeler, but still helps out part time and sits on the Board of Directors. He stays current and still delights in flying.

Hopkins doesn't just promote aviation safety for others – his personal safety record is spotless. FAA recently recognized his 10,600 hours of safe flight by awarding him the Wright Brothers Master Pilot Award for more than 50 years of accident-free flying, traversing a lifetime of service to aviation needs around the world. When speaking with him about his excellent accomplishments, he mentioned what's most important to him – although he's now a Master Pilot, he's always been the Master's pilot.

Article for *Safety Net* by Joe Hopkins

Moody and MSI – Reflections from the MSI Founder

Moody Aviation's desire to add to their flight training staff a person with experience on the mission field led me to make the transition from Mission Aviation Fellowship to Moody Aviation in Tennessee in 1972.

During the next ten years I helped develop pre-field check-outs and furlough refreshers for other mission pilots as well as for Moody students. I saw that many smaller missions did not have safety departments such as larger missions had and pilots returning home on furlough after three or four years of being on their own were often "rusty" in some flying skills. This realization led me to the conviction that safety services should be available to small missions also.

The first Moody Aviation Safety Seminar was held in 1979 and was a cooperative effort between training schools and aviation mission agencies. We came to realize that **continuing education** was essential to safe operations and so continued the Moody seminars every two years. We also felt it very important that safety concepts and thinking become ingrained in students from the beginning of their training so they would **make safety a way of life**.

Increasingly obvious was the belief that an **independent agency** could best serve the many agencies operating airplanes—where individuals might be more willing to share real issues with a trusted "outsider" than they would with colleagues from their own mission.

With some sense of trepidation, I broached the subject with my boss, Dirk Van Dam, who was the Moody Aviation Director. He was warm to the idea and became totally supportive of the effort. This led me to seek counsel from many mission leaders about the idea of forming an independent agency solely dedicated to safety education and services. The response was overwhelmingly positive. The only thing left to do was the risk to resign from the faculty of Moody Aviation and launch **Mission Safety International**. MSI was incorporated in 1983 and now, thirty years later, I am truly convinced it was the right thing to do.

While working out the details of the new organization, and beginning overseas travels for safety seminars and audits, Moody provided office space for MSI for years until we moved into another facility. I continued my role as Safety Coordinator for Moody in Tennessee until they moved to Spokane, Washington.

I'm happy to say that, though Moody has changed location, they have not changed their goal of producing as safe a mission mechanic and pilot as possible.

Joe Hopkins History

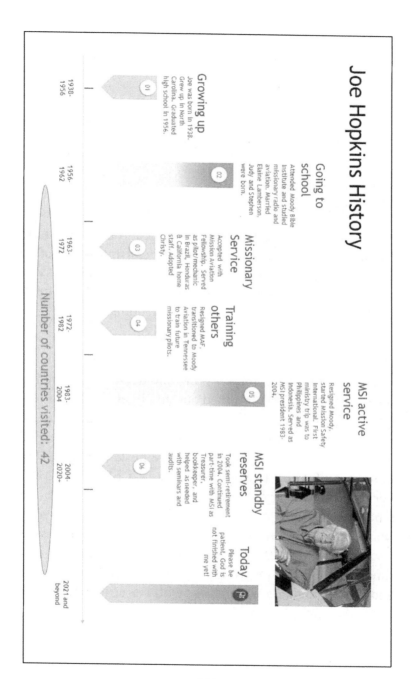

Growing up
Joe was born in 1938. Grew up in North Carolina. Graduated high school in 1956.

01 — 1930-1956

Going to school
Attended Moody Bible Institute and studied missionary radio and aviation. Married Elaine Lamberson. Judy and Stephen were born.

02 — 1956-1962

Missionary Service
Accepted with Mission Aviation Fellowship. Served as pilot/mechanic in Brazil, Honduras & California home staff. Adopted Christy.

03 — 1963-1972

Training others
Resigned MAF, transitioned to Moody Aviation in Tennessee to train future missionary pilots.

04 — 1972-1982

MSI active service
Resigned Moody, started Mission Safety International. First ministry trip was to Philippines and Indonesia. Served as MSI president 1983-2004.

05 — 1983-2004

MSI standby reserves
Took semi-retirement in 2004. Continued part-time with MSI as Treasurer, bookkeeper, and helped as needed with seminars and audits.

06 — 2004-2020+

Today
Please be patient. God is not finished with me yet!

07 — 2021 and beyond

Number of countries visited: 42

A NEW CHAPTER

It was a dark and stormy night...

We were huddled in the basement room of the farm house trying to be attentive to the constantly updating weather reports of local tornado activity while at the same time listening to the howling wind outside. Lightning flashes and peals of thunder kept interrupting.

But let me back up. I had not attended the EAA (Experimental Aircraft Association) annual fly-in at Oshkosh, Wisconsin for six years and decided I wanted to once again attend. As it turned out, Jon Egeler, who usually goes as MSI representative, was unable to go this time, so it worked out for me to go. When Elaine and I first attended about thirty-three years ago, we were hosted by a lady by the name of Mary Grace Viste. She and Elaine hit it off very well, and Mary always welcomed us to stay with her whenever we attended EAA, which we did. Meanwhile, Mary married. After twenty-one years, her husband passed away in early 2020. When she heard I was coming this time, Mary invited me to stay with her again. Her daughter and three grandkids were living with her at this point, but she had plenty of room.

We, having both lost our spouses about five months apart, spent several hours the first two nights after EAA reminiscing and remembering our recent year's caregiving challenges as well as our past good times together. It was the third night, with the threat of tornadoes, which drove all of us to the basement. It was a long night with very little sleep—but fortunately no structural damage from the storms—that led to more in-depth talks. By the end of the week, both Mary and I knew that something special was developing, though totally unanticipated by either of us.

Long story short, we were married several months later and feel that this new Joseph and Mary chapter has real potential for interesting and fulfilling ministry opportunities yet to come—but then, that's another story...

Mary and Joseph, married September 25, 2021

Joseph Guy Hopkins, Jr.

Birth: October 2, 1938
Death: --- *To Be Revealed*
—Currently Living in the Dash—

1938—???

Made in United States
Orlando, FL
21 July 2022

20048642R00143